POCKET
THERAPY

POCKET THERAPY

Mental Notes for Everyday Happiness, Confidence, and Calm

Sarah Crosby

ST. MARTIN'S
ESSENTIALS
NEW YORK

Published in the United States by St. Martin's Essentials, an imprint of
St. Martin's Publishing Group

POCKET THERAPY. Copyright © 2022 by Sarah Crosby. All rights reserved. Printed in Canada.
For information, address St. Martin's Publishing Group, 120 Broadway, New York, NY 10271.

www.stmartins.com

The Library of Congress Cataloging-in-Publication Data is available upon request.

ISBN 978-1-250-82006-8 (trade paperback)
ISBN 978-1-250-82007-5 (ebook)

Our books may be purchased in bulk for promotional, educational, or business use. Please contact your local bookseller or the Macmillan Corporate and Premium Sales Department at 1-800-221-7945, extension 5442, or by email at MacmillanSpecialMarkets@macmillan.com.

Originally published as *Five-Minute Therapy* in the United Kingdom by Penguin Random House UK.

First U.S. Edition 2022

10 9 8 7 6 5 4 3 2 1

To Louise, Ger, and Claire—
and to all those who show others what it is to feel safe

CONTENTS

INTRODUCTION

Hi.

It's you! You're here.

I'm so glad you are.

Welcome to *Pocket Therapy*. Chances are you're curious about who you are and you're looking for a guide to start exploring that further. The exploration of self is essential to creating and maintaining happiness, confidence, and calm in our lives. So if that's something you're looking to cultivate, you're in the right place. It's an interesting thing to think about really, isn't it? Who am I? What does that dreaded phrase "Just be yourself" even mean? What does it mean to be "authentic?"

Before you and I get into what *Pocket Therapy* is, allow me to share with you one of my earliest memories of being told who I am at the age of seven. Perhaps you can recall your own experience of this, too?

As the school year came to an end and parents faced the looming reality of two whole months of uninterrupted episodes of *Sabrina the Teenage Witch*, many of us kids found ourselves back in our primary school under the guise of a "Craft Camp," now joined by students from other local schools.

So, in the heart of the rainy Irish summer, we gathered in Ms. Monaghan's classroom, where I sat with my friend Claire, waiting for the fun to commence.

"Tell us about yourselves!" a slightly erratic coordinator bellowed to the congregation from the front of the room.

At first, nobody spoke, and then all at once a cacophony of sound arose from the mass.

"I'm Paddy!"

"I'm six."

"My phone number is—"

It was an onslaught to the senses.

"I'm Sarah!" rang out, as all other noise came to a close. I shrank back, wary of having identified myself.

"OK, let's sort you by names!" boomed the coordinator, who proceeded to retrieve a lengthy roll of nametags from Ms. Monaghan's drawer.

For the next fifteen minutes, the coordinators zigzagged between us all, asking each of our names, scribbling them on stickers, and placing these on our T-shirts.

"There you go, Sarah. That's you."

I looked down at the tag, all gaudy loops and swirls. I guess it isn't so bad having to wear this for the day, I thought.

"OK, everyone. Now sort yourselves into groups of the same name!"

I looked up to see horror on every face. Was he mad?! I know some people here, but others are from the school down the road! I don't know them! They're practically alien, I thought.

They shuffled us about for the next few minutes, until we found ourselves disjointed from our original pairings. I stood with three other just-as-morose-looking Sarahs—one without an "h," but I had no drive left to argue semantics.

I gazed around. The Aoifes and Aislings looked to be in the majority (both evidently popular girls' names in Ireland at the time). My friend was now part of her own considerable tribe. I cast a sympathetic look to the rogue names among us, until they grouped Delilah, Anastasia, and Tobin together under "Miscellaneous."

Panic began to rise inside me. I was to spend the rest of my week with three girls I didn't know simply because of a labeling I had no choice in.

I don't like this, I thought, and so, mustering up what courage I had to rally against the system, I bid farewell to the Sarahs, peeled off my nametag, and crept over as stealthily as I could to the Claires, who were both welcoming and happy for the numbers, and with whom I sat for the remainder of the day.

I was terrified of authority as a child and yet, I just felt I couldn't blithely spend my week teamed with others united by a random label that we had no say in.

Although in this instance I "rebelled" against the categorization with gumption (as well as a belly full of anxiety), there are many other times in life that I've accepted much more unhelpful labels, whether imposed by myself or others. While the instance above was, on the surface, relatively harmless, the bigger point I'm getting at is this. We tend to take on board and absorb what we are told of who we are, which means that experiences like this can define our sense of self from an early age.

Throughout my adult life, in both my personal experience and in my experience as a psychotherapist, I've come to the understanding that a large part of discovering who we really are comes from unpeeling the tags we've had attached to us along the way, and choosing to explore what lies beyond the limits of the labels.

3

Right off the bat, let's put our cards on the table. *Pocket Therapy* is many things, but I want to be clear from the start that it isn't a new therapeutic approach that will magically fix all your problems in five minutes. Nor is it a replacement for therapy or any mental health support. *Pocket Therapy* won't spoon-feed empty promises or sell a quick fix. Nor will it do the work for you—to help you feel happier, more comfortable, and more confident in yourself. Sorry to be the bearer of this news, but I thought it best to start this relationship with openness and honesty!

What you *will* find in *Pocket Therapy* is, hopefully, more meaningful. A journey of self-discovery. A peeling-away of the aforementioned labels. An exploration into selfhood. A chance for therapeutic insight into your own life, away from all the noise of social media.

This book is full of accessible, bite-sized information, which you can choose to dip into or read right through in the order it is presented. With any luck, you'll find the thoughts and ideas within the pages to be a source of insight, reassurance, comfort, and support.

"Take 5" features throughout the book offer simple but effective practical exercises for you to try in any spare moments you can find or create. And at the end of each chapter you'll find "Mental Notes" that encourage you to take five minutes at the close of each day to reflect on the key themes just discussed in that chapter.

While I bring to these pages my expertise as a psychotherapist, *you* bring the knowledge of who you are and the world you live in. So, this book isn't a definitive guide on "How To Be Yourself The Way I Tell You To." It's an open invitation to embark on a journey of selfhood.

It's something to turn to if:

* You feel curious and want to get to know yourself a bit better
* You feel a bit (or a lot) lost, and are looking for more clarity
* You feel a bit shit, and would like to feel better
* You're not sure quite what you want, while everyone else seems to be steaming ahead with certainty
* You want to feel happier, more confident, and calmer
* You're open to exploring the ways we drift away from ourselves and the ways we can get back to our true inner selves.

It's an exploration of the many different parts of who we are and how we are, in the hope we come to recognize the pieces of ourselves that need embracing and the other parts that no longer fit the person we have gradually become.

You will come across lots of buzzwords such as attachment, boundaries, self-care, and compassion in this book, so if terms like this make you feel queasy in any way, I suggest consuming this content with a mug of builder's tea.

We've reached a sort of online saturation point with many mental health terms. I even find *myself* suppressing a grimace at overused words such as "boundaries" from time to time (the whole of Chapter 6 is about "boundaries" by the way). Eventually I had to address this aversion within myself—due to the risk of writing off certain key messages simply because of overexposure to particular words. There's a reason we're using such terms more and more: the conversations that they allow are both important and necessary. So I invite you to park any reservations you may have about such "jargon" along with my own.

My hope is that within the pages that follow you'll find easy-to-digest insights into not-always-easy-to-digest topics—reflections, practical guidance, exploratory questions, mental notes, and various other tools that you can use to more fully explore yourself.

Whether you currently have a good sense of who you are or you're feeling a little lost in life, you can use this book to reflect, deepen your understanding of certain parts of your experience, and hopefully begin to recognize and break old patterns, and also to create new ways of being.

Establishing, or recovering, our sense of self is a journey of accumulated choices that each of us makes. Nobody can hand our sense of self to us. So while this book will offer insights, reflections, and suggestions that, together, can make a major difference to your life, in my experience, just *reading* about such things is rarely enough to bring about lasting change. Insight raises awareness, but *real change* requires work, action, risk, compassion, vulnerability, and patience with your process.

So it will serve you well to really engage as best you can with the reflections, practices, and mental notes as you work your way through the book. I would suggest keeping a journal as you move through each chapter. And know that if you're not feeling it some days, allow that to be OK, too.

Each chapter will consider a different aspect of the relationship with the self:

1. Self-Discovery—How to Be Yourself
2. Exploring Attachment—How to Create Meaningful Relationships
3. Self-Talk—How to be Kinder to Yourself
4. Recognizing Triggers—How to Understand Your Reactions
5. Self-Regulation—How to Soothe Yourself

6. Setting Boundaries—How to Practice Genuine Self-Care

7. Reparenting—How to Heal Yourself

8. Going Beyond the Self—How to Be a Good Friend

Before you venture through the chapters on your own inner journey, two key questions that you might consider asking yourself right now are:

* How do I feel about myself?
* How would I like to feel about myself?

Take your time. This will give you a sense of what you would most like to get from the pages ahead of you.

THE NEED FOR THIS JOURNEY OF SELF-DISCOVERY

Below are some reasons it can be worth going on the journey of self-discovery that this book offers:

* We could nearly all do with cultivating a more calm, conscious relationship with ourselves.
* Loving ourselves can feel difficult. To promise that this book will set you off on a continuous love story with yourself would be naive. Like any relationship, your relationship with yourself is constantly in flux. Everyone, and I mean *everyone*, will have off-days when they feel like a bit of an impostor, when they

scroll through social media and feel body-conscious or when they simply don't feel like facing the world. Self-discovery introduces the notion of neutrality. We're neither in the depths of self-scrutiny, nor are we continuously striving for transcendence. Within neutrality lies acceptance. And while this might not initially seem like something to aspire to, after taking up the exercises over the coming pages, I hope you'll notice that you start to become less hard on yourself, steering away from the overly critical, tyrannical inner bully (more on this in Chapter 3!) and stop setting the bar at anything less than complete self-love.

* If you deliberately avoid addressing your self-relationship, you may repeat patterns that you have subconsciously learned or inherited. At one stage in your life, these patterns may have been necessary and/or helpful but, over time and through overuse, such patterns can end up holding you back, rather than helping you.

* Your relationship with yourself often reflects how you operate in your interpersonal relationships. Feeling good about who you are will complement every other relationship in your life. For this reason, cultivating self-awareness is, in fact, a selfless act.

* When you are curious about the beliefs you have, you become more conscious of the moments when limiting beliefs might be "running the show."

* Bringing attention to your relationship with yourself doesn't stop feelings from arising. It simply allows you to bring intention to how you would *like* to respond to these, rather than having knee-jerk reactions from a place of anxiety or anger.

* Cultivating a conscious relationship with yourself allows you to experience the richness and fulfillment that other relationships can bring to your life. Your sense of worth begins to build and because of this, you will start feeling more secure in yourself. When we know our worth, we know we're worthy of the right sort of love.

Whether you dip into these pages every once in a while, or use the notes daily to further personal insight, I hope they bring you a growing sense of connection, safety, and ultimately, empowerment. Inward and onward …

1.
Self-Discovery

HOW TO BE YOURSELF

"Knowing yourself is the beginning of all wisdom."
Aristotle

The phrase "Just be yourself" is something we often hear from well-meaning loved ones before things like a job interview or a date. But it's a phrase that I have personally struggled with, as being yourself can be a tricky task if you're not sure who that person is.

"Be myself?" But what if others don't like that person? What if they don't want to hire that person? What if they don't want to *date* that person? I have a better plan: I'll suss out who I think they *want* me to be and I'll give them that! Good idea, right…? I certainly used to think so.

It took quite some time for me to realize that "be yourself" doesn't equate to morphing my personality to suit the person I'm with. Don't get me wrong, it can be fine to claim in an interview that we understand the minutiae of Excel or Adobe if we know that that's what is needed, but there's more of our *deeper* sense of self at risk if we are willing to alter our core values and behaviors depending on the company we're in.

Being yourself isn't something we can suddenly "switch on." We don't wake up one morning and decide "Hmmm … I might start being my full, authentic self today," like it's been hanging at the back of the wardrobe, just waiting for the right weather. Rather, it is an ongoing process based on lots of choices that we make daily, so try not to worry if you don't yet feel that you've got it all sorted.

In my experience as a therapist, someone with this concern comes into my office almost every day. So you're by no means the only one who "can't get it right" while everyone else can.

WHAT IS THE SELF?

Before we think further about self-discovery, let's take a moment to consider our concept of what the "self" actually is. The foundations of our sense of self form early in life, shaped and influenced by a multitude of experiences. Some of these include:

* Early exchanges with our caregivers
* How loving and reassuring these relationships were
* How self-aware our primary caregivers were
* The expectations and wishes of those around us
* The environment we grew up in
* The emotional stability of the household we were raised in
* The schooling we may have received

WHO ARE YOU,
BENEATH
EVERYTHING
YOU'VE BEEN
TAUGHT YOU
HAVE TO
BE?

* Interactions with our peers
* The societal valuing of certain identities over others, such as the entrepreneur, the athlete, the model, etc.

From the growth of mainstream self-development and an ever increasing focus on being the most productive (i.e. "successful") version of ourselves we can be, a notion of an *ideal* self has emerged—of a person who is so self-aware that they can rise above anxiety, doesn't feel triggered by anything, wakes at 5 a.m. each morning to meditate, and is, generally, wise beyond belief.

But this notion of a "perfect," static self is a mythical one. A fantasy self that is fixed, predictable, and consistently consistent.

I don't know about you but, to me, it actually sounds a bit boring, a bit robotic... And it's certainly unrealistic! Yet many of us might be battling with this notion of the mythical Self—as if it's what we should all be striving for.

And when we break this down, it's understandable that we might think this. After all, how do we *know* what parts of us are, or could be, our true selves? And what parts of us are constructs that have formed in response to our experiences in life so far?

The Self is not just one thing; it is formed of many moving parts. And yes, that can mean that our awkward teen self is as much "us" as our mature, grown-up self.

We will never know and understand everything about ourselves—although in a time that seems rather obsessed with productivity and optimization, it can be easy to feel pressured to try to reach this goal.

As such, it can be useful to take a moment now and again to simply check in with what self-discovery expectations you're placing on yourself. Do they need tweaking to be more realistic? After all, you weren't formed to fit inside the parameters of a neat little box, whether it be of your own creation or someone else's.

You may at first be resistant to the notion that some parts of yourself will always remain a mystery. So you might need time to come to terms with the idea of not knowing every aspect of who you are.

It's useful to remember in this respect that we all have finite energy. And when we dig our heels in, determined that things be a certain way, we use up a lot of this energy; energy that could be better used on getting out and exploring the world.

To discover and uncover who we are, it's important that we let go of the idea of the self as a destination, or as one concrete, all-seeing, all-doing, all-positive entity.

We're all just human—full of both light *and* shadow. We're going to make mistakes. More than that, we *need* to make mistakes.

Self-discovery is about continuously ebbing and flowing toward who we are. So it's important to give yourself permission to go out and discover.

It can be difficult to "just be yourself" if:

* As a child, individuality and self-expression weren't encouraged
* We've experienced abandonment in our lives
* We were subjected to bullying, either growing up or in adult relationships
* We were criticized for showing the weird and wonderful sides of ourselves that we all have
* We don't fit the mold of what society wants of us.

MAKING A CONTINUAL CHOICE TO BE OURSELVES

Learning to be ourselves can be some of the hardest and bravest work we ever have to do. It is something that many of us think about a lot—as we continue to meet, confront, and create different aspects of ourselves every day. As such, it's useful to see the process of continual discovery as a blessing, rather than a curse; a salve rather than a suffering.

Each and every day we're presented with multiple opportunities either to move toward our true selves or to hang back and take the path of least resistance.

Sometimes the choice is pretty straightforward, such as deciding what to listen to, what new show to binge-watch on Netflix, what to read, or what to eat. These are decisions that pose little risk to our sense of self, particularly if we're making the decisions when alone.

However, other opportunities present much greater challenges in terms of feeling into who we truly are, so feel more intimidating. For example, we might have a different opinion to our partner and battle with whether to "just go along with it" or speak up. We might disagree with the behavior of a parent but feel it isn't our place to say something. Another's expectations of us may clash with our own view of our self, but we feel a pressure to collude …

It took several years of inner work for me to be able to gain this perspective on my sense of self but doing so was liberating. When you consider your sense of self as a fixed destination, or a list of milestones, you can easily fall into the trap of labeling yourself in some way, such as "boring" or "behind in life." When you think of the self as in constant movement, on the other hand—as a daily "becoming"—you introduce the possibility of inviting in some playfulness, some curiosity, and some compassion.

In the end, we always risk more by trying to be someone we are *not* in our daily interactions than by being ourselves. While on the surface each small decision may seem minor, the cumulative effect is ultimately one of self-loss.

WHAT IS SELF-LOSS?

Self-loss is the feeling of not knowing who we are, or a sense of disconnection from ourselves. This may be a long-standing disconnection that we experience throughout our lives, or something more sudden.

Signs of Self-Loss:

* Feeling unfulfilled with your life as it is
* Distrusting your own judgment
* Behaving impulsively and seeking instant gratification
* Struggling to make decisions on things that wouldn't have bothered you before, then second-guessing the decision you finally make
* Becoming more critical of yourself and others
* Being drawn to co-dependent relationships (relationships in which one partner is dependent on the other partner, who in turn, needs to be needed)
* Finding it difficult to establish a deeper connection with those around you.

When we experience self-loss, we might find ourselves thinking things like:

I don't know who I am. I don't know what I like. I don't know what I want to do. I don't know who I want to be. I don't know what my life is about or what I want from it. I feel panicked, unmotivated, worried, scared, indecisive, numb even. I feel like I'm failing. I feel like everyone has their shit together, except me. I feel behind.

This can be frightening, so it's important to address any feelings of self-loss as soon as they arise.

TRIGGERS FOR SELF-LOSS

Self-loss can be caused by a number of factors, most commonly:

* Relationships
* Family units
* Grief
* Trauma
* Changing roles

WHEN A
RELATIONSHIP ENDS,
WE GRIEVE MORE
THAN THE LOSS
OF A PERSON.

WE'RE GRIEVING THE
LOSS OF EVERYTHING
IT REPRESENTED TO US
+ WHAT WE BELIEVED
COULD HAVE BEEN.

Relationships

Sometimes we become so deeply enmeshed with another person that, before we know it, we've lost all sense of who we were before the relationship with that person began. In cases like this, we tend to prioritize the needs of our partner over our own needs. And sometimes the relationship can become controlling or abusive in some way, causing us to step away from our friendships and activities in order to keep the peace.

Sometimes, by society's standards, a certain romantic relationship might not be viewed as much of a relationship at all because, for example, it wasn't "Facebook Official," or it lasted little under a season; and yet, when it ends, we feel distraught. Conversely, another relationship might last for years, yet we don't feel as bad as we expect after it ends as we've retained some kind of sense of ourselves in it.

Here's the thing about relationships—time cannot quantify the effect particular connections can have on our lives. Relationships represent more to us than the sum of their parts. This becomes particularly clear when we find ourselves unable to understand post-break-up heartache, especially if the relationship was brief or the break-up was initiated by you.

Relationships represent safety, aliveness, a rough draft of a possible future. So when we enter into one, we start to entertain the idea of what it might be like to let this person in fully. When a relationship ends, we therefore grieve more than just the loss of the particular person in question. Instead, we grieve the loss of everything that relationship represented to us and everything we believed it could have come to represent. So remember to be gentle with yourself in such times.

The Family Unit

All children need what is referred to in psychotherapy as a "secure base" in order to grow into adults with a balanced sense of self.

When caregivers provide us with this secure base, we can explore our wider environment in the knowledge that we are not only safe, but that, on our return from our explorations, we will be met with presence, sensitivity, comfort, and love.

Unfortunately, however, there are many people whose parents never show up for them in this way, whether deliberately or otherwise. Some parents are doing the very best they can but are struggling with their own issues. Others are absent—either physically or emotionally, or both. And, sadly, others are sometimes just cruel or unpredictable. As our sense of self is formed in early childhood, any of these examples of an "insecure base" can leave us with a faint sense of self.

Early negative interactions often become lessons we internalize. So, for example, if a child's cries are met with verbal or physical aggression, the child may begin to associate reaching out for help with pain. As a result, they may begin to deny the emotional parts of themselves that give rise to the aggression in the other. Having to reject parts of the self in childhood in this way is then likely to give them a propensity toward disconnection and self-loss in adulthood. And so a pattern created in childhood journeys with us into adulthood; often early childhood trauma can extend far into adulthood, even if our memories do not.

Grief

The death of a loved one can uproot even the surest of selves. Grief tends to shake us to the core, leaving us feeling completely and utterly adrift. And while this sense of loss is often to be expected around the passing of those in our inner circle, a similarly deep sense of loss can come as a shock when it's about, for example, someone we weren't particularly close to—sometimes someone we had never even met. Indeed, the death of a pet, for example, so habitually negated by society, may be one of the most profound losses we've experienced thus far. We spend so much of our time avoiding the topic of death and its inevitability, not just individually but in society at large, that when someone in our acquaintance passes, our usual avoidance of the reality of death is rudely interrupted.

We may find that after a death, we begin to question our own life choices and priorities. What once seemed so important suddenly might seem frivolous, making a certain disconnection from our sense of self inevitable. We might also find ourselves frustrated at those around us for their inconsequential hang-ups, which can feel prickly and distressing. But remember, the thistles will lessen with time.

Although it may not feel like it right now, when some time has passed, looking anew at our priorities and taking the chance to reset our sense of self can be empowering, if we let it. Author Mitch Albom said it beautifully in *Tuesdays with Morrie*: "Death ends a life, not a relationship." While this is true for the relationship with the loved one who has passed, it is also true of the relationship you have with *yourself*. You're not gone or truly lost; you're just hidden underneath grief, taking care of your pain as best you can.

Trauma

Trauma is a response we have to any event or experience that overwhelms our capacity to process and cope. It impacts how we think, feel, perceive, and process, affecting us physically, emotionally, psychologically, socially, and often also spiritually—causing us to experience a form of self-loss.

What is highly distressing and traumatic to one person may not cause the same response in another. For example, the loss of a pet or a sibling moving away will cause very different reactions in different people. This is why understanding the effect of an event on someone is much more significant to determining trauma than the details of the event itself.

Validation of our experience of trauma is integral to our capacity to reconnect with ourselves but this can sometimes be incredibly difficult for us to do. Often we might have invalidating thoughts such as "I should be doing better," "I should be over this already," "Others have it worse," or "They went through the same thing and they're fine." Note the element of comparison at play in many of these self-dismissive thoughts.

What's important to remember here is that we all experience trauma differently, we all heal differently, and our responses do not indicate either strength or weakness.

How we process trauma depends on many factors, such as our biological make-up, the nature of the event, and access to support. Our response to trauma is our brain and body doing what they need to do in order to keep us safe, so if you're feeling a disconnection from yourself as a result of trauma, know that what you're experiencing is a rational reaction. Next time you catch those invalidating claims sneaking in therefore, remind yourself that your process is uniquely your own and cannot be compared to another's. Even invisible wounds require care.

Changing Roles

From an early age, we receive all sorts of messages, whether consciously or subconsciously, about what's "cool" and what's not, what's "good" and what's not. We'll look further at roles in the family later in the book, but for now let's think back to our school years, where we were inundated with social information.

You can study for your exam, but it's not a good idea for people to know that you have.

Butterfly clips are the height of style and you have to get on it, quick.

It's not OK to fancy her!

Be Yourself! But no ... not like that!

What is acceptable here? What could get me thrown out of this group? There's safety in belonging, so, as children, we learn from a young age what interests and inclinations could become a barrier to our inclusion. And as we filter all this information, we learn what roles to play to our advantage. These roles aren't always hugely different to our "real" selves; sometimes they're just slightly different or muted versions, where our eccentricities are dialed down, for example.

Sometimes it's even the loss of one of the *roles* we play that can leave us feeling disconnected from who we are. As I came to terms with my diagnosis of inflammatory bowel disease, for example, I felt a loss of autonomy and also of my role as "The Drama Kid," who was at home on stage. I was now "The Crohn's Kid," "The Sick Kid." Similarly, if we end a long-term relationship, we might feel unsure who we are outside of the role we have been playing in it. If we finish college or a particular job, we might find ourselves lost without the structure of the academic year or the office environment. Some parents feel guilty when they have newborns for missing aspects of their pre-parent selves. And other parents feel anchorless when their children leave home. A loss is a loss, and all losses can be felt keenly.

Take 5: Me, Myself, & I

Start exploring your own experiences of self-loss up until now by asking yourself the following questions:

* Which forms of my "self" did I need to be growing up?
* Who did I need to be in order to be accepted by my friends?
* Who did I need to be loved by in my relationships?

Alternate the "did" above with "do," place them in a current context, and see how your answers look now.

Ways We Avoid Addressing Self-Loss:

* Drastically changing who we are depending on who we're with
* Mimicking others

* Going along with others' expectations
* Becoming unhealthily attached within our relationships
* Not forming or expressing our own opinions
* Automatically accepting the opinions of others as the "right" one
* Saying yes when we mean no
* Numbing out through overworking, substance use, exercise, etc.

AVOIDING SELF-LOSS

I tried to avoid confronting the feeling of loss within myself for many years. I wasn't conscious of it at the time, but I grafted to avoid it. I was unable to see that all I was doing by avoiding it was postponing dealing with it. There are some necessary pains in life that we can't escape but I was willing to try, because confronting them would mean having to work toward accepting the person that I really was—something I really didn't want to do because, ultimately, I detested who I was.

I avoided, avoided, avoided. Until I couldn't avoid anymore. I hit that low point—the one you hear people speak about, but you never think will happen to you. The enormity of my own sadness and anxiety overwhelmed me. I couldn't sleep. The anxiety attacks began. And my usually quite dormant Crohn's disease kicked into high gear. When we stop listening, eventually the body screams.

Bringing your fears into focus might seem risky, as if paying attention to them will amplify them, make them even worse. It's only human that we want to distance ourselves from unpleasant emotions and sensations. Why would we choose to

AVOIDANCE
PROVIDES AN ILLUSION
OF CALM, BUT IT'S A
TEMPORARY LOAN
AT BEST (AND THE
INTEREST RATE CAN BE
EXTORTIONATE)

intentionally welcome discomfort? But, as Carl Jung said, "What you resist not only persists, but will grow in size." And this was essentially why I found myself in a therapy session at the age of twenty-three and why I had to eventually face rather than flee my feelings.

Perhaps you relate; perhaps not. I don't believe we need to get to our lowest of lows to address our sense of self-loss, but I've found that awareness often brings with it discomfort. Not all discomfort need be negative though. Sometimes it's a sign of change—a form of growing pain.

Things to Remember About Avoidance:

* Avoidance provides an illusion of calm but it's a temporary loan at best (and the interest rate can be extortionate)
* Trying to keep fear and discomfort out of our awareness is draining
* We can't "let go" if we never look at what we've kept in
* Spending energy on avoidance depletes our vitality
* Resistance generally creates more unease than the thoughts that we're resisting.

DISCOVERING AND RECONNECTING

The process of discovering and reconnecting with ourselves isn't a switch that we flip, nor is it a finish line that we run or cartwheel across. There are no shortcuts to self-discovery; the journey itself is where the gold lies. The clue is in the term. Self-discovery is finding; it's curiosity; it's unpacking and unpicking. The good news is that, given you're reading this, you've already begun the process. So, going forward, allow yourself to engage with the practices with the honesty and presence you're already applying.

Discovery isn't a means to an end.

So give yourself permission to soften, to just be, and to enjoy the process, when you can.

Take 5: Becoming Aware of Your Choices

It can be useful to consider the process of self-discovery in terms of movements that we make on a daily basis, so ask yourself:

* Which choices and actions bring me closer to myself?
* And which choices and actions do the opposite?
* Am I moving toward my true self, or drifting away?

NOTICING AND NAMING

The process of noticing and naming our emotions can bridge the gap between what we're thinking and what we're feeling. When naming, try stating what you're feeling. So instead of "I am angry," say "I am feeling angry." "I am anxious" becomes "I am feeling anxious." "I am stressed" becomes "I am feeling stressed." And so on. The step from "I am this" to "I am feeling this" allows you to recognize that you are not exclusively that emotion and gives you space to observe the feeling, rather than be it. It also serves as a gentle reminder that the emotions you're feeling are temporary; a comfort when what you're feeling is anything but comfortable.

Noticing and naming what we're aware of, both in our body and mind, may seem trite, yet many people avoid doing it due to the discomfort it can involve.

Here's a tip I received from a mentor of mine: Place a small sticker somewhere in your room or on the back of your phone. When you notice it, check in with what you're aware of in your body. Begin by asking: What is it I'm aware of feeling right now? As time passes, we naturally become more accustomed to the sticker and less aware of its presence but I can safely say that now and then, many years after sticking the little blue dot on my bookshelf, it still serves its purpose for me.

Take 5: Check In with Yourself

One of the most accessible and underutilized tools we have at our disposal is our ability to check in with ourselves and just observe. This doesn't have to be complicated. We can do it right now:

* How am I feeling? Perhaps I feel tired, hungry, or anxious?
* What sensations do I associate with this feeling that have made me aware of this? Jot down your answers in a journal.

KEEP PLAYING

As children, we're given permission to play. We test the waters. We don cloaks. We play with who we are. "Is this a bit of me, or isn't it?" And, as an Aunty to six niblings, I can vouch that hell hath no fury like the child who has been asked to stop playing!

But somewhere in our early twenties, society seems to expect us to dial our playfulness down, often with a final crackdown around the thirty mark.

"No more playing for you! You should know who you are now that you're a 'grown-up,' and any trying, testing, or playing around with who you *might* yet be is likely to be deemed a quarter- or mid-life crisis."

Playing becomes a sign of "immaturity." A sign of "failure." So we lose the ability to play and to explore. Yet this leaves little room for movement or growth—and we weren't born to stay the same forever. Just as our bodies change, so do our selves. Some parts we outgrow. Some parts we bring with us throughout life. Others we discover as we age …

Take 5: Playing with Life

Take a moment to answer the following questions for yourself:

Is there something I have always wanted to try but haven't yet? It could be dancing, acting, a beginner's course in Finnish!
Is there a way of exploring this? Even a little? Allow yourself to trial. Allow yourself to error. Start to play with life again.

RECOGNIZE OPPORTUNITIES

Every day we make choices to move closer or further away from ourselves. Part of the self-discovery process is allowing ourselves to become more curious (without judgment!) about these daily choices that we make.

I used to find "small talk" particularly painful. Not because of the predictable topics of conversation, but because of how I felt about myself after it. My true self didn't show up in small talk at all. I'd say things I didn't really believe but thought was "what people say." I'd find myself dropping in a piece of gossip because I was so keen to fill the silence. I'd walk away and verbally berate myself for the way I'd participated in that moment. The truth is that I was acting out of a fear of rejection and a place of anxiety; what if they didn't like me? What if they thought I was weird? I was so busy trying to anticipate what the other person wanted or would admire that there was no room for me to show up in the conversation as myself. Meanwhile, I drifted further and further away from myself.

Simply becoming aware of this habit changed how I participated in those moments. My newfound awareness helped me to be able to see the wood from the trees, as only when you become aware of common feelings and behaviors, can you start to question their causes.

The original script of my inner monologue about small talk was along the lines of: "Oh god! Make it stop! People are going to find out how stupid I am—and how weird I am. What I just said makes NO sense at all. Did I really just say that and agree with that?! Did I agree AND make a bad pun??? Why are you like this? Seriously, Sarah, just go home. It's official. Everyone hates me."

You can see why I often left social situations in a panic. However, I can now see that I missed what was actually an opportunity to just connect with others on a genuine level. I had been so overwhelmed worrying about the ways I was going to get the interaction wrong that I couldn't see the chance to connect. Having this insight about the potential for connection, whether you are in a small-talk scenario, a meal with your family, a work meeting, or any other situation in which we find ourselves triggered and drifting away from our authentic self, can be a real catalyst for change.

CREATE A SUPPORTIVE SCRIPT

We can use the space that this insight offers us to become more inquisitive about what is happening, even when we feel an intense pull to drift into familiar patterns in order to please or appease someone else.

Clearly my negative internal monologue about small talk wasn't doing me any favors socially, but in terms of my self-discovery, once I started to see what was actually happening, it turned out to be a treasure chest. Once I was able to recognize my eagerness to please and my subsequent self-criticism, I wrote it down. Having the thought process on paper allowed me to see it for what it was and respond to it, not in my usual manner by verbally slating myself, but with more softness and kindness.

So I've now changed my script about small talk to something much more positive and self-supportive: OK. Here we go. In moments of small talk, I usually feel I agree too much or say things I don't mean. That's OK. I understand some of the reasons for this. I have concerns, but I don't need to prove my worthiness to anyone. Even if I notice I've slipped into agreeing again after this encounter, it will be OK. I'm learning. One step at a time. So I can go easy on myself. They've asked me something and I notice I feel I should go along with their opinion…but what do I actually think? I don't know right now, so I'll say just that and give it some thought afterward. Breathe. Slow down. Take your time. You're doing well. You're safe.

Creating a supportive script like this for yourself about an area that you struggle with is not a quick fix; it's more sustainable than that. By engaging with it, you suspend your cynicism (I'm Irish so, trust me, I know that can be hard), which can provide a powerful anchor for anxious moments. In essence, it turns you simultaneously into both your own hype-man and your own comfort blanket, gently guiding you back to your true self.

Take 5: Edit Your Script

Either take a pen and paper or open up a blank note on your phone (side swipe your notifications for the moment) and…

* Using the above example as a guide, write out your "Original Script." This doesn't necessarily have to be about small talk, like mine was. It could be about anything, e.g., how you speak about your body, your capabilities, your work, how you parent. Choose what topic feels right to you.
* Write down some opportunities to connect with yourself or others (depending on your chosen topic) that you have in your day/week. Are there any you may have overlooked because of your original script? (These might include moments when you're looking in the mirror, when you're sitting outside, or when you're at your laptop reviewing your work. It might

include moments with friends, family, acquaintances, classmates, or even people you encounter on the journey to and from work.)
* Can you identify what worries and fears lie underneath these thoughts? Once you've given some attention to this, write an alternative caring and supportive version of the script in response to the original fear-based one, and use it to anchor you during challenging moments.

CARVE OUT SOLO TIME

Another really important thing to do on the journey to knowing yourself better is simply to spend a little time by yourself. Before I lose you, I'm not suggesting you either *Eat, Pray, Love* your way around the world or Witherspoon your way across the Pacific Coast Trail. (Although let's be honest, who hasn't thought of it?)

Spending some time with yourself may sound like the last thing you want to do. And the idea of solo time may even feel frightening. You might associate solitude with isolation, but solitude and loneliness aren't the same thing.

We tend to worry about what will confront us in the stillness of alone time. With the rise of individualism and increasing emphasis on creating our own empires, stillness is regularly conflated with stagnation. If we're still, then we're not working toward the production of something "greater," something "better," something more lucrative. This, of course, is a myth, but the implicit messages we receive from society cast long shadows.

Making some regular time for yourself is a deeply nourishing practice and a great way to cultivate a strong sense of who you are, away from life's usual distractions. In a world where we overwork, spread ourselves thin, distract ourselves with social media, podcasts, and other external stimuli, and fill every pocket of silence with noise, solitude is something we have to practice.

Yet we all have the *capacity* to sit with ourselves, so it isn't about an inability, a laziness, or not having the time. Instead, most of us fear that by sitting with our feelings, something uncomfortable will bubble up to the surface that we won't be able to control. We all walk around with undigested emotions, undigested anxiety, and sadness. This might not come from "big things"; it could just be the slights we receive daily, such as moments of misunderstanding or disconnection with people close to us. Allowing dedicated space for the emotional accumulations of your day therefore mitigates the longer-term storm that tends to accompany avoidance.

Solo time doesn't have to be spent sitting in meditation, although meditation is a wonderful practice. You can use the time to do anything you truly want to do.

Ideas of Ways to Spend Your Solo Time:

* Flex your creative muscles by doing some drawing or writing
* Engage in self-reflection with the mental notes for this chapter
* Go for a walk (preferably without your headphones)
* Feel into nature; take off your shoes and socks, and plant your feet on the grass or soil
* Create a morning ritual—rise, stretch, make a tea, journal, set your intention for the day, and select an affirmation from the list on page 115

* Wean yourself off technology by creating pockets of time in the day when you're device-free. Begin by giving yourself five minutes in the morning; then extend this when possible.

CONNECT WITH OTHERS

While it's important to practice the art of solitude, it's also important to prevent feelings of loneliness. There's a big difference between the two.

More than ever before, a lot of people in today's busy world are experiencing feelings of loneliness. Even if we live in the heart of a city, surrounded by people, it's possible to feel lonelier and more isolated than we do when in solitude. Studies continue to emerge detailing the effects of loneliness on both our physical and mental health, with younger adults reporting loneliness more than any other age group. The social spaces where we once connected are dissolving, and sparking up a conversation face-to-face with a relative stranger is often met with suspicion and reservation, especially in city commute scenarios.

This becomes a bigger problem when society starts wrapping self-isolation in a cloak called "self-care." Stay in. Cancel. Cut off. Of course, there are times when these measures are absolutely necessary for our wellbeing, whereas in other moments it is connection that is essential.

After all, we can discover a lot about who we are when we're in the company of others. If you circle back to the original script and the supportive script above, you can see just how much of our patterns, our reactions, and our curiosity emerge by simply being in the presence of others.

It can sometimes be difficult to nudge yourself out the door. It's becoming less "natural" for us to step outside and let the fresh air blow the cobwebs away. But self-discovery doesn't have to solely be a solitary endeavor. In fact, it can't be. Occasionally, we need to nudge ourselves back toward connection—with others as well as ourselves.

Take 5: Give Yourself a Moment

How am I feeling?

Do I feel lonely?

What would be best for me right now?

When was the last time I went for coffee with someone?

How busy have I been in work lately?

Tune in to your intuition. Although you might want to spend the day beneath the duvet, what is your gut telling you?

CHEAT SHEET:
WAYS TO CONNECT
WITH YOURSELF

SELF-REFLECTION
JOURNALING
MEDITATION
MOVEMENT
READING
CONVERSATION
NOTICING
EXPERIMENTING
MUSIC
THERAPY

MENTAL NOTES

Take five minutes at the end of each day for a month to reflect on the following:

* Where was there an opportunity to connect with myself today?

* How would I like the relationship with myself to feel?

* What would help in moving myself toward this tomorrow?

* What three things am I grateful for today?

After the month, you'll have created a treasure chest of information about yourself, including actionable steps in terms of how to move closer to who you really are.

MOVING FORWARD

Hopefully, this chapter has provided moments of insight. You don't have to remember them all. They're in there somewhere, distilling and processing, resting and realigning. A quote by the American essayist Ralph Emerson in his book *Self-Reliance* states, "In every work of genius, we recognize our own rejected thoughts." Let's extend Emerson's philosophy beyond celebrated genius. How many times have you read something online and sent it to a friend? Or come across a line in a book and hastened to scribble it down? Or heard a lyric that broke your heart in two? We discover ourselves in the words we read and the words we hear every day. Keep this in your heart as you journey forward.

GENTLE REMINDERS FOR CHALLENGING MOMENTS

* It's OK to feel uncertain. You're growing your capacity to be with discomfort.

* You are doing your situational best. That looks different for us all depending on the day and the moment.

* You have had difficult times before. And if you're reading this, you're already raising your level of consciousness. Breathe deeply.

* You've started the process of self-discovery. Acknowledge that.

* Nobody has all their shit together (regardless of how it looks on social media). Everyone is figuring out who they are on a daily basis. You haven't lost who you are. You're already whole; parts of you just need time to heal.

2.
Exploring
Attachment

HOW TO CREATE MEANINGFUL RELATIONSHIPS

"The quality of your life ultimately depends
on the quality of your relationships."
Esther Perel

Ever wonder why you attract the people you do? Why you get so upset when your partner doesn't reply to a text or why the same arguments keep cropping up? Perhaps you've noticed you really want to be in a relationship—that is until you're in one? Or why your friend is ready to move in with someone after the second date whereas it takes you two years to utter "I love you?" We all have very different types of relationships with the people in our lives.

EXPLORING STYLES OF ATTACHMENT

If you've been to therapy, chances are that the notion of attachment has come up in some shape or form—and for good reason. In essence, attachment is how we relate to other people, and our "attachment style" is responsible for checking the safety and availability of the people in our lives. It is our relationship blueprint which sums up the type of emotional bond, or connection, that we tend to feel with others.

Understanding our attachment style is helpful as it:

* Affects how we feel, think, and behave in every relationship we have
* Informs our relationship with intimacy and our narrative surrounding romantic, friendly, and familial relationships
* Impacts the way we approach conflict and resolution
* Offers insight into how we felt as a child
* Shows how we might defend against emotional connection
* Shines a light on relational wounds that need our attention.

Attachment styles form in childhood as a result of the relationship a baby has with its caregiver. Attachment is essential for relational and emotional development. We're born with an innate drive to form an emotional bond with the caregiver that provides everything essential to our survival: food, warmth, and safety.

The style of this attachment is formed through nurturing, play, and, most importantly, how responsive a parent is to the needs of the baby. When a child cries, how does the parent respond, for example? With soothing coos, or with frustration and a raised voice? Does the parent look into the child's eyes? Or are they absent, or distracted by their phone?

The cumulative effect of these interactions determines how steadfast a child's sense of security is. When an infant can see and feel their caregiver responding consistently, lovingly, and quickly, the child learns they can trust the people responsible for their care and survival. This ultimately cements the foundation of a secure attachment.

Attachment styles can be categorized into four groups:

1. Anxious
2. Avoidant
3. Disorganized
4. Secure

However, these styles, much like our sense of self, aren't static. Although they form in childhood, numerous factors can affect them throughout the course of life.

These factors include all sorts of both positive and negative life experiences, including but not limited to early friendships, encounters with bullying, moving home, illness, financial security or insecurity, the death of or separation from a loved one, healing experiences in intimate relationships, personal achievements, addiction, abuse, neglect, commitment to self-work, and the relationship we have with our therapist, if we have one. Negative experiences cause us to feel less secure, while positive experiences enable us to heal and feel more secure. No attachment style is necessarily "bad." Nor is it a justification for any kind of negative or abusive behavior. "It wasn't me, it was my attachment style" won't get you very far.

Although there isn't a wrong attachment style to have, the hope for many of us is to work toward a secure bond as this will reduce the amount of emotional and relational pain that may hinder us from living a fulfilling life.

It's important to know, however, that the attachment style we each develop in childhood isn't a choice that we make; it is simply something formed to keep us safe. So with that in mind, it is good to approach the information that follows with compassion, curiosity, and a willingness to work toward healing—as we explore which attachment style we feel that we ourselves have.

Take 5: Check in with Yourself

Before we delve further into the different types of attachment, take stock of where your thoughts are right now. Perhaps you're racing ahead, wanting to know more. Maybe you've already picked which attachment style you *hope* to have. Ask yourself:

* What assumptions am I making?
* Can I keep an open mind as I read ahead?
* Am I open to being surprised or mistaken?
* Can I separate what I would like from what *is*?

It's important to stay open and stay curious.

I. ANXIOUS ATTACHMENT

The hallmark of "anxious attachment" is a craving for intimacy. The words "clingy" and "needy" are often used when talking about people with this attachment style, but the reality is more nuanced.

Within anxious attachment, we can oscillate from a slight feeling of loneliness to molding parts of who we are to "fit" whatever relationship we're in, to sending a stream of texts to an unresponsive friend.

The phrases "I feel a little lost in my own company" or "I seek a lot of reassurance so that I can feel safe in relationships" may feel suited to the experience of those with anxious attachment.

People with this attachment style tend to be highly perceptive, which is a great skill to have. It allows you to read a room, pick up on the emotional temperature of others, and instinctively know when those close to you are feeling a bit low and may need a helping hand or an empathetic ear.

This ability to observe and sense is powerful. And yet, it also enables you to pick up on subtleties from the environment and use them to propel fears or interpretations about how others feel about you.

A trigger for anxious attachment is the real or perceived withdrawal or rejection of another. For example, when someone is quiet, a person with this attachment style may interpret this as someone not liking them. They may think the quiet person has grown weary of them or that, somehow, they've done something "wrong," which would explain why they've withdrawn.

PEOPLE WITH ANXIOUS ATTACHMENT...

ARE PERCEPTIVE TO SUBTLE CHANGES IN OTHERS

ARE SENSITIVE TO SIGNS OF WITHDRAWAL [REAL + PERCEIVED]

CAN HAVE A NEED FOR NEAR CONSTANT CLOSENESS + CONTACT

FAUX WITHDRAW WHEN PARTNER DISTANCES

CAN FEEL SUSPICIOUS ABOUT A PARTNER'S ACTIONS + EXPERIENCE INTENSE BOUTS OF JEALOUSY

All attachment is a spectrum rather than an absolute. So the level of anxiety one person feels may be very different to someone else with the same attachment style.

In addition, the level of anxiety we feel in our friendships might feel very different to the level of anxiety we feel in romantic relationships. Attachment responses can feel as strong as a screaming match or be experienced as just a subtle hum of apprehension, running in the background throughout our day.

An activated anxious attachment style can sound like:

"I love you more than you love me"

"I want to spend ALL of my time with you"

"I feel anxious when I'm alone"

"You're going to leave me"

"You're going to cheat on me"

"Have I done something wrong?"

"Are you mad at me? Are you OK?"

"Why aren't you texting back?"

"You don't care about me"

Do these resonate with you? If so, what might you add to the list above?

How Anxious Attachment Forms

There are many factors beyond childhood that can influence attachment style. However, the initial blueprint of an anxious attachment style is linked to a childhood in which a caregiver was:

* Unpredictable in their availability
* Inconsistent with their praise and/or punishment
* Not in tune with individual needs
* Encouraging of helplessness
* Discouraging of autonomy.

In the absence of reassurance, insecurity builds in us, as children. When our needs are then threatened, as adults, and our attachment system becomes activated, it can result in safety-seeking behaviors, sometimes also referred to as "protest behaviors."

Safety-seeking behaviors are actions carried out with the intention of restoring a felt sense of safety. It is worth noting that what we *believe* will provide us with a feeling of safety is not always correct; sometimes this "safety" is a temporary illusion, or we're mistaking safety simply with what is familiar.

For the anxiously attached, safety lies in closeness and dependence. Although safety-seeking behaviors are a part of every relationship, it is the frequency and intensity of these behaviors in people with anxious attachment that can overwhelm, particularly if actions result in a negative response from others.

Safety-Seeking in Anxious Attachment

Safety-seeking behaviors among the anxiously attached are any attempts to re-establish closeness and to elicit a response from other people.

While some of the behaviors (see following list) may seem counterproductive to achieving closeness, remember that getting a negative response is still a response, as it's an indication that the other is still there. They haven't left, at least not fully. The hope of the anxiously attached is often that by either bombarding or withdrawing, the other person will reach across the divide and restore a sense of safety.

As such, while the anxiously attached person might appear withdrawn or "unphased" by whatever is going on, inside they are likely to be experiencing a whirlwind of emotional turbulence.

Safety-seeking within anxious attachment can involve:

*   Bombarding others with messages and calls, and frequently checking to see if they're online
*   Ignoring, withdrawing, or pretending to become engrossed in something else, such as a book or social media
*   Making plans with others in order to look "in demand"
*   Attempting to elicit jealousy through insinuation, such as by mentioning someone flirted with us today or speaking about an ex. (While discussing crushes, relationship history, and sexual experiences are a part of any healthy

relationship, it can become detrimental to the overall safety in the relationship if spoken about with the intention of making another jealous.)

* Threatening to leave if things don't get better.

Take 5: Explore Your Safety-Seeking Behaviors

Take a moment to reflect on your own safety-seeking behaviors by asking yourself:

* What do I recognize as my main safety-seeking behaviors—in romantic relationships; with family; and with friends?
* Do I therefore seem to be anxiously attached? Or might I fall into one of the other categories of attachment?

Healing Anxious Attachment: Where to Start

For the anxiously attached, the key to healthier relationships lies in cultivating inner safety and independence.

Within romantic relationships, this work is easier when a securely attached person is present, as the consistency of a secure attachment helps us to start trusting in the reliability of others. If an anxious person is with an avoidant, it is harder as the avoidant tends to confirm the anxious person's negative beliefs about themselves: as the avoidant withdraws, the attachment activates, reinforcing old theories they have such as "I'm too much," "I'm too clingy," and so on. If you find yourself in a relationship with someone who also has an insecure attachment, don't feel disheartened. The relationship isn't doomed—it just means that each of you will have to work a little harder in order to communicate your needs in a healthy way and create a sense of safety.

However, developing a sense of safety isn't only available to those in romantic relationships. Every type of relationship has the potential to bring about healing. Whether in a relationship or single, we can all benefit by investing our energy and time into the development of a range of different types of relationships, whether old friendships, new friendships, group activities, or whatever else. You deserve to surround yourself with individuals who support your growth, rather than condemn it. Cultivating a sense of self-trust will also help with this, and we'll look at that more in Chapter 7 on Reparenting.

As difficult as it can be to acknowledge how your attachment style shows up in your life, the good news is that you're not stuck operating from your early safety system. So there's no need to blame and shame the younger you, who had no choice in the matter. Instead, it's good to start trying to understand. And if you don't understand quite yet, simply keep practicing curiosity. Focus on where you go from here and your commitment to educating yourself further.

All our actions as adults are our own responsibility. So to challenge any problematic behaviors, whether attempting to make others jealous, threatening to leave a relationship, or whatever else, we need to firstly be aware of our behaviors, address what worries or concerns may be driving them, and begin to learn and practice self-regulation techniques, which we will discuss later in the book (see Chapter 5).

2. AVOIDANT ATTACHMENT

People with "avoidant attachment" may initially come across as mysterious, guarded, or a closed book. They may be experienced by others as emotionally unavailable, insensitive, or "commitment-phobes" which, depending on where we lie on the attachment spectrum ourselves, may all seem true to us.

Avoidant attachments prioritize self-reliance and independence. And while a sense of agency and assurance are healthy aspects of selfhood, it is the degree to which avoidants contain their needs that can begin to cause pain for both themselves and others.

Avoidant attachment behaviors can involve:

* Both consciously and unconsciously keeping others at arm's length, due to a lack of trust
* Ghosting, canceling, and cutting ties with others when it suits
* Carrying over past pain to present-day relationships
* Meeting your *own* needs in a relationship, rather than having to rely on others, as this would risk the pain of them not delivering.

Avoidance is a *defense* mechanism. But shielding oneself from the possibility of true connection means that the road to emotional intimacy is a tough one for avoidants.

After all, nobody is needless, so when a desire for true connection comes to the surface, people with this attachment style generally have to disconnect from these vulnerable parts of themselves. When they're unable to disconnect from this desire entirely, they tend to berate and bully themselves for having a need for connection in the first place. And, subsequently, they may criticize a partner who is open and comfortable in communicating the very needs that they deny within themselves. Talk about a vicious circle!

An activated avoidant attachment style can sound like:

* "I don't need anyone"
* "I don't like asking for help"
* "I don't need anything from this relationship"
* "I need space"
* "I feel trapped"
* "I don't feel like anyone really knows me"
* "Why are you so needy?"

Do these resonate with you? If so, what might you add to the list above?

PEOPLE WITH AVOIDANT ATTACHMENT...

PLACE PARTICULAR IMPORTANCE ON AUTONOMY + FEAR LOSING IT

CAN FEEL OVERWHELMED BY THE EMOTIONAL NEEDS OF OTHERS

HAVE A HARD TIME WITH COMMUNICATING EMOTIONS

CAN MISTAKE OTHERS' IMPERFECTIONS AS RED FLAGS

OFTEN FEEL UNSAFE WITH INTIMACY + CLOSENESS

How Avoidant Attachment Forms

Experiences throughout our lifetime can influence how secure or insecure we feel in relationships. For example, harmful experiences such as bullying and emotional abuse later in life can erode the foundation of a secure base formed when we were children.

However, avoidant attachment is generally linked to a childhood in which a person had to disconnect from their bodily needs or minimize these needs as they arose, such as a need for comfort and affection. It tends to spring from a childhood that involved a caregiver who:

* Was unpredictable or frightening
* Was unresponsive, discouraging, or disparaging of sharing emotions
* Withheld affection
* Made them feel ignored or rejected.

This pattern is then carried through and repeated in adult relationships.

Safety-Seeking in Avoidant Attachment

Our attachment style unconsciously ticks away in the background but there are certain situations that can activate avoidant attachment in particular. This could be, for example, anger expressed by someone close to us, real or perceived controlling behavior, or excessive contact or "neediness" displayed by another.

As with anxious attachment, when avoidant attachment is triggered, we engage in certain safety-seeking behaviors in an attempt to re-establish a sense of security within. But in contrast to the anxiously attached, who find safety in closeness and dependence, the avoidant finds safety in distance from the other person involved.

An avoidant's safety-seeking behaviors, sometimes also referred to as "deactivating strategies," are therefore any actions or thoughts used to create distance between you and the other. In essence, the purpose of these strategies is to protect and shield the self from potential emotional pain. For the avoidant, who on some level always feels alone, constant contact plays into a fear of losing autonomy as well as a fear of being manipulated.

Safety-seeking within avoidant attachment can involve:

* Repeatedly "failing" to respond to someone
* Prioritizing work and hobbies over quality time with a loved one
* Being purposefully vague about plans
* Shutting down in conflict
* Daydreaming about the benefits of "single life" or the ex that got away
* Idealizing relationships besides the one we may be in, with the grass always a few degrees greener elsewhere
* Focusing on the faults of others as time goes on
* Feeling the right partner would just "get" us.

All of the above can happen in any relationship. It would be a mistake to think that a secure relationship has consistent and static levels of intimacy. Relationships naturally change over time—sometimes we grow apart and other times we may find we've been in four different relationships with the same person over time. An avoidant, however, puts in place walls and all sorts of other defenses to manage their growing anxiety and to shield from potential heartbreak.

In short, they unknowingly create a self-fulfilling prophecy, because, as others become frustrated with their behavior and reject them, it allows them to interpret the response as evidence that others can't be trusted!

Understanding how safety-seeking behaviors can contribute to the pain that avoidants try so hard to escape is a key part of healing from the psychic scar tissue of our relational wounds.

Healing Avoidant Attachment: Where to Start

Working toward healing attachment wounds means getting really curious and honest about the intentions behind our actions, which is a difficult thing to do.

Avoidants can be reluctant to look at the ghosts of relationships past. But unpacking these, as well as questioning the stories we attach to certain relationships, is crucial. So try to notice the patterns that you're reluctant to delve into. Start small, and build from there.

For example, if a partner reacts in a certain way, what story do you attach to what just happened? It might be "They expect too much of me, I have to get out," "This is where they become disinterested so I'm going to leave," or "This won't last." Becoming aware of your own stories will help you to understand how your past experiences are still affecting your life today. Examine and question your narratives and see what patterns emerge.

Take 5: Explore Your Safety-Seeking Behaviors

Take a moment to reflect on your own safety-seeking behaviors by asking yourself:

* What do I recognize as my main safety-seeking behaviors—in romantic relationships, with family, and with friends?
* Do I therefore seem to be avoidantly attached? Or might I fall into one of the other categories of attachment?

Avoidants tend to keep a lot to themselves. So to counteract this, it's helpful to practice sharing small pieces of what you're feeling, or something personal about yourself, with people you trust.

Sometimes, connection requires a leap of faith. Putting yourself out there is likely to feel highly uncomfortable for avoidants, so, rather than judging the "success" of your sharing based on the response of the other person, recognize the risk you took and how big that is for you. You may not get the reaction you want, but you will have practiced vulnerability—a big step toward changing a long-standing pattern.

Activated avoidants will often require some space before they will feel able to fully engage. So, if you recognize that you're an avoidant, try to communicate what it is you need when you see this happening. For example, in conflict, this might sound like

"I can see things are escalating here. Could we take fifteen minutes apart and come back to discuss it then?" In circumstances outside of conflict, you may feel spread thin, increasingly frustrated, and confused about why you're feeling this way. In this case, again, try to lean into curiosity and communication, whether it's with a friend, family member, or partner. It's OK to ask for support in identifying what your needs are, because we all have them.

3. DISORGANIZED ATTACHMENT

"Disorganized attachment," also sometimes called "fearful-avoidant attachment," is the rarest of the attachment styles, affecting roughly 7 percent of the population.

At times, it is also referred to as the "come here–go away attachment"—and for good reason, as it is seen as a combination of anxious and avoidant attachment.

People with this style of attachment desire intimacy and connection, but at the same time are terrified of it. So as a relationship with someone who has disorganized attachment deepens, the person tends to freeze, dissociate, flee, or all three.

People with this style of attachment tend to have low self-esteem, display highly erratic behavior, be prone to intense emotional storms, and have a rocky sense of self.

While some of us may recognize aspects of ourselves in these descriptions, it doesn't necessarily mean that we have disorganized attachment. This seems particularly important to mention as more often than not, people tend to believe they have a disorganized attachment. While we have a primary attachment style, we will also display traits of other styles depending on the situation and the company we're in. So while we may display characteristics of both anxious and avoidant attachments, as you'll read below, a disorganized attachment style is linked with early trauma, inconsistent and volatile treatment from our primary caregiver, as well as a profound lack of a sense of self.

How Disorganized Attachment Forms

Disorganized attachment is linked to a childhood that involved a caregiver who:

* Was unresponsive and stone-faced
* Didn't meet the needs of the children in their care
* Was frightened and/or frightening
* May have been prone to displays of anger, neglect, or abuse
* May have deeply struggled with unprocessed trauma and their own mental health.

Children in the care of someone like this would have found themselves frightened of them yet desperately reliant on them for their comfort and wellbeing. And being raised in such an environment would have led to a combination of neediness and hypervigilance in adulthood—where there is a simultaneous desire for intimacy and an extreme mistrust and fear of it.

PEOPLE WITH DISORGANIZED ATTACHMENT...

DISPLAY A COMBINATION OF ANXIOUS + AVOIDANT TENDENCIES

OFTEN HAVE AN UNSTEADY + LOW SENSE OF SELF

STRUGGLE TO REGULATE EMOTIONS

ALTERNATE BETWEEN FEELING NEEDY + FEELING DETACHED

DEEPLY DESIRE INTIMACY BUT FIND IT DIFFICULT TO DEPEND ON OTHERS

TEND TO FIND THEMSELVES IN STORMY, VOLATILE RELATIONSHIPS

The Cycle of Disorganized Attachment

Look at the Disorganized Attachment Cycle on page 69. Have you been in this loop? Whether you're the initiator or the recipient, this cycle highlights one of the ways disorganized attachment can show up in relationships, causing both confusion and hurt to all.

Disorganized attachment can involve:

* One day feeling the person beside you is the greatest, and the next, feeling overwhelmed and claustrophobic
* Wanting to take a risk on intimacy, like most others, but being scared of a hurt you feel that you would never recover from
* Putting up walls when a relationship starts to feel "real"
* Creating both physical and emotional distance, only to panic when the distance created is all too effective, as you haven't escaped the hurt you fear.

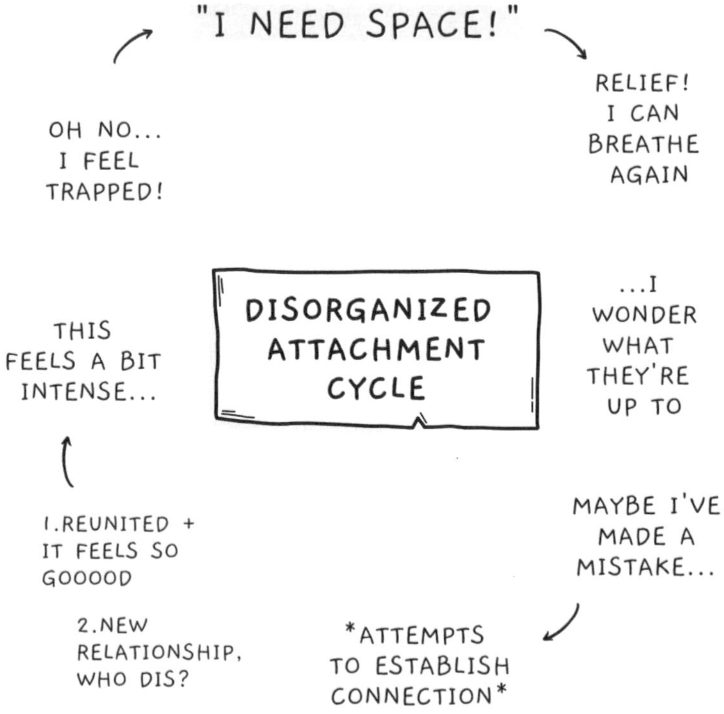
"I NEED SPACE!"
RELIEF! I CAN BREATHE AGAIN
...I WONDER WHAT THEY'RE UP TO
MAYBE I'VE MADE A MISTAKE...
ATTEMPTS TO ESTABLISH CONNECTION
1.REUNITED + IT FEELS SO GOOOOD
2.NEW RELATIONSHIP, WHO DIS?
THIS FEELS A BIT INTENSE...
OH NO... I FEEL TRAPPED!
DISORGANIZED ATTACHMENT CYCLE

Take 5: Explore Your Response to Love

Ask yourself:

* What happens when I love someone?
* What happens when someone loves me?

If you have a secure relationship with intimacy, you are likely to answer in a positive way, such as "When I love someone or someone loves me, I feel motivated, warm, content." However, if you have disorganized attachment, and a negative history of intimacy as a whole, you are likely to think something more like: "When I love someone or someone loves me, I lose myself / they ask too much of me / I get hurt…"

Healing Disorganized Attachment: Where to Start

Navigating a disorganized attachment style is immensely difficult. First and foremost, if not already in therapy, consider reaching out to a psychotherapist or trauma therapist, particularly if dissociation (a disconnection from your body, thoughts, time, or place) is present.

Therapy can provide the healing, secure base we require to work through trauma and relational wounds in a safe and guided way.

If in therapy as someone with disorganized attachment, notice how the cycle in the image opposite appears with your therapist. Do you cancel or "forget" your sessions? Do you feel dependent on your therapy one moment and feel reluctant to go the next? Perhaps you do something similar with friends? Identify your patterns and create a conversation around this with your therapist.

In cases where therapy isn't an option, seek communication and conversation elsewhere, such as through support groups or close friendships.

When a child is feeling sad, hurt, or angry, it's not our role to convince them that they don't feel this way. The same goes for how you deal with your inner child (the younger you). So try to stand back, look at what's happening objectively, reflect, and offer comfort. Consider what has made the insecure child in you go from happy to anxious. From calm to impulsive. Insight does not guarantee change. But it creates the possibility for change, if we allow it. Use the information in the image on page 69 to assist with this tracking.

The process of healing can take an uncomfortable route and, unfortunately, you can't hitch a ride to the end; you have to drive yourself. So notice the bumpy inner journey that you most likely feel hesitant to embark on if you fall into this category of attachment. It asks for honesty, self-compassion, and patience amid all the growth. And the sooner we can come to terms with this, rather than in any way resisting the discomfort to come, the more of our finite energy we will have to invest in healing.

4. SECURE ATTACHMENT

If you grew up in an environment in which your needs were mostly met, without you having to struggle for care and attention, it's likely that you will have grown up with a "secure attachment."

People with a secure attachment style generally feel that people are good. They can trust and connect with others easily. And they have a good sense of who they are.

But even if you identify with one of the other attachment styles, it's helpful to understand what a secure attachment looks and feels like. After all, how can we know if our attachment is healing if we don't know what a secure one looks like in the first place?

I'd now like to do a spot of myth-busting. It's all too easy for us to romanticize what we feel an ideal relationship "should" look like; what it should be. We can choose to see another couple (perhaps made up of two people with secure attachments) and believe that their sex life is both plentiful and acrobatic, that their emotional life is a dream, and that the only reason they might ever raise their voices is to tell each other how in love they are over the din of the shower before they each skip off to a challenging yet high-achieving day at the office. But rationally, we know better than this …

Having a secure attachment does not equal "fantasy relationship." People in securely attached relationships, like all others, have arguments, need solo time, experience hurt, anger, and disappointment. The distinction between a secure attachment and the other three attachment styles covered in this book is in the individual's sense of safety within themselves. How secure you feel will show up in your level of self-worth, your emotional response to situations, your capacity to focus on issues at hand, and your ability to self-soothe. So it's important to be realistic about this.

PEOPLE WITH SECURE ATTACHMENT...

ENJOY + FEEL COMFORTABLE WITH EMOTIONAL INTIMACY

EXERCISE HEALTHY DISCERNMENT WHEN IT COMES TO TRUST + DISCLOSURE

HAVE A STRONG SENSE OF OWN BOUNDARIES + RESPECT THE BOUNDARIES OF OTHERS

HAVE THE CAPACITY TO ACCEPT RESPONSIBILITY FOR MISTAKES WITHOUT SHAMING THEMSELVES

ARE ATTUNED TO THE EMOTIONS OF OTHERS

Markers of Secure Attachment

* **Staying Present**

    A person with a secure attachment doesn't get overly hung up on the "What Ifs" with a partner or other people. They're able to be present, without feeling the need to control all outcomes.

* **Emotional Availability**

    A person with a secure attachment tends to shy away from emotionally distant and emotionally volatile people. They have a good sense of self-worth and what they bring to the table. They don't feel the allure of the highs and lows of a relationship because they recognize that these aren't needed for them to feel seen or loved.

* **Ability to Manage Impulses**

    All relationships involve elements of jealousy, anger, conflict, and the like. But secure attachment individuals have a high ability to reflect on conflict and uncomfortable feelings without becoming distant or defensive. Arguments therefore tend to focus on processing frustration and understanding the hurdles in communication, rather than becoming a means to hurt one another or to "be right."

* **Capacity to Apologize**

    Whether it's forgetting date night or making a double booking with friends, a person with a secure attachment is usually able to offer up a genuine apology, without overanalyzing their own reliability or projecting anger and blame onto others. A securely attached person will hold themselves accountable, without diving headfirst into an evening of self-disparagement.

* **Balance Within Conflict**

Insecure attachments are often at their most obvious during conflict. They can cause tunnel vision during arguments and make you forget the qualities you love in your partner. People with secure attachments, on the other hand, have a high capacity to simultaneously hold space for what could seem like contradictory emotions, so they could, for example, simultaneously feel both anger and love for their partner.

* **Consistency**

When we identify someone as emotionally volatile, it can be difficult to determine what their response might be at any given time. Their mood, their reactions, and how they treat a partner can vary greatly, affecting the ability of their partner to trust, enjoy, and feel safe within the relationship. Even the mood of a person with secure attachment will fluctuate (our attachment doesn't make us immune to the human experience!). However, those with secure attachment will show their love in a more consistent manner, through reliability and trustworthiness. Just like that of the child seeking security from their caregiver, it is not enough to be told we're safe. Safety is something we have to experience.

Take 5: Know Your Attachment Style

Now that we have covered the various attachment styles, where on the attachment spectrum do you believe you fall? If you're not yet sure, here are a few sample questions that you can use to guide your reflection:

* The majority of the time, how do I respond in conflict?
* How do I feel about intimacy?
* How comfortable am I sharing my feelings with someone close to me?

Feel free to add your own questions to get a fuller picture of your own attachment style and how you might like to develop this.

Developing a Secure Attachment

Reading about attachment can be difficult. Although it can bring a bucket full of insight, inevitably it will also bring into focus other truths that may be uncomfortable. Trust me: it will be worth it in the end though.

Remember, as we've said before: you aren't stuck with your attachment style. Even if you identify as high up on the anxious or avoidant scale, this doesn't have to be your final destination.

Changing your style takes work, deep reflection, and accountability, but it is entirely achievable. And if you're connecting with what you're reading here, the odds are already in your favor. The potential to heal lies in every one of us, so recognize this possibility that you hold in your hands right now. It's up to you what you do with it.

Healing attachment isn't something we do by ourselves. By its very nature, it involves examining our internal representations of relationships and working toward more genuine connections with others.

The narrative we most often hear in regard to healing attachment involves entering into a relationship with a securely attached individual and learning from their display of support and trust. But healing doesn't have to happen this way or even come from a romantic relationship. It can exist in *all* relationships. The loving support of a therapist; honesty and connection within friendships; communicating in a new way with a parent—all such relationships can bring levity to intense feelings that come up when we experience unmanageable internal states.

Healing requires us to be willing to reflect on ourselves unreservedly—with curiosity, with honesty, and, crucially, also with kindness. This is what really matters.

No matter how loving and available a partner is, they will at some point fail to meet us when we need them, as they, like us, are just human. Occasional failure at empathy is the reality of life, and the hallmark of a securely attached person is the ability to trust the undulating waves of the relationship. We won't find a person who doesn't trigger us at all but we can develop an internal stance of the loving parent for our scared inner child in order to help us through (see more on this in Chapter 7 on Reparenting).

It's important to recognize that healing someone else's attachment goes beyond our capabilities and responsibilities. We can't lug someone up the garden path of healing. However, we *can* walk alongside them by being open and understanding, while maintaining our own self-respect and boundaries.

MENTAL NOTES

Take five minutes at the end of each day for a month to reflect on the following:

* What attachment triggers and safety-seeking behaviors came up for me today, if any?

* What emotions was I aware of feeling at the time? And what did I feel in my body?

* When could I have expressed my relationship needs more clearly today? What would that have sounded like?

* Going forward, what is one way I can move toward connection in my relationships? What would that look like?

After the month, you'll have a trove of material about how you operate within relationships, including actionable steps in terms of how you can enhance things further.

3.
Self-Talk

HOW TO BE KINDER
TO YOURSELF

"You will never speak to anyone more than you speak
to yourself in your head. Be kind to yourself."
Unknown

Have you ever caught yourself berating something you've done? Perhaps you've been speaking meanly to yourself for simply being yourself? Or putting yourself down for not being *smart-funny-slim-good-successful-whatever else* enough? Do you find you compare yourself to others? Or make assumptions that others don't like you? If so, don't worry. You're not alone!

In the pages that follow we'll look at ways that we can start to change this, including getting to know what stories we've created in our own heads about ourselves, how we talk to ourselves on a day-to-day basis, thinking traps that we tend to fall into, and how we can start to heal our own self-talk so that we generally feel better in ourselves. So let's get going…

OUR STORIES ABOUT OURSELVES

We all craft and create a story in our own head about who we are. The tale is usually elaborate and multifaceted. It includes some fundamentals such as our name, age, background, the job we do, and so on. And it can also include the various roles we play in life, the relationships we've cultivated, what we like, what we loathe, what we hope for in the future, and much more.

When we hold our self-story, or self-description, lightly and with interest, it can assist us in expressing and explaining aspects of who we are and what we would like out of life.

When, on the other hand, we start to hold on to our story too tightly, we can begin to merge with it and feel as if we are *solely* this story. And this can swiftly conjure up a whole host of issues, as we confuse our thoughts for being the very core of who we are.

If the story in our head is a critical and self-deprecating one, then the more attached we become to it, the more we risk believing that we *are* what the negative elements of the story dictate—I *am* my story, so I am incapable, ugly, stupid, a failure, or whatever else.

This is then likely to start affecting our behaviors, which means, for example, that we might not feel confident enough to go for the job we really want; we might

MENTAL NOTE

WHEN WE WEAVE
OURSELVES INTO
THE FABRIC OF OUR
STORY, IT GIVES THE
NARRATIVE INFLUENCE
OVER OUR MOOD
+ OUR BEHAVIOR

not speak up when we've got something to say; we might shy away from people or situations where we risk being vulnerable; and so on.

Issues can also arise if we have too positive a self-story. "But wait!" I hear you say, "I thought speaking more kindly to myself was what I should be aiming for?" Yes, hopefully by the end of this chapter you will identify areas of your life that could benefit from a positive change in the way you speak to yourself. However, if we hold on too tightly to a very positive self-story, we risk leaving no room for anything outside of this.

Say, for example, that we hold on too tightly to the idea of being self-sufficient. Self-sufficiency is, of course, often very useful, as it can bolster self-trust, self-confidence, and independence. But what happens when we need help or support? This is, of course, inevitable, as nobody is needless.

If our story begins and ends with "I am self-sufficient," it leaves no room for the help we're in need of. So instead of reaching out, we might spread ourselves thin and wear ourselves out. Instead of seeking support, we might bottle everything up and become unhappy. The initial positive story of "I am self-sufficient" becomes a burdensome one of "I *have* to be self-sufficient."

Likewise, we run into problems when our ongoing self-story conflicts with our current life experiences. For example, what happens when someone who normally plays the "therapist" role to other friends—and who has started to fuse with this story about themselves—begins to burn out and no longer has the energy to be the patient listener that others rely on?

This situation might lead to the person thinking "I'm the listener, so I shouldn't be feeling this way. I need to try harder to be there for them." And, if they, in turn, then try to live out this story, they will most likely just get more and more exhausted, and potentially also resentful. We can see from all this then that when we weave our sense of self too tightly into the fabric of the story we tell ourselves in our head, it can give our self-story too much influence over our behavior.

However, if we can start to bring more conscious attention to both the positive and negative anecdotes about *ourselves* that have become embedded in our head, we will greatly benefit, as we will be able to identify and address the parts of our story that we've become overly attached to and that may therefore be thwarting our ability to live as full a life as possible.

Take 5: Hold Your Story Lightly

Take a few minutes to consider what the main self-story in your own head is at the moment. Then as you meander through this chapter and the rest of the day ahead, hold this story lightly and with interest. Are there certain snippets you could stand to loosen your grip on?

OUR INNER VOICE

Whether we are conscious of it or not, most of us have an inner voice. A voice that maintains an internal running commentary throughout our days. A constant form of "self-talk" or monologue.

It's generally not in the soothing tones of David Attenborough but even so, it is something most of us have.

Sometimes, this voice can be supportive and affirming, calming our anxieties and celebrating our wins. However, on other occasions, the internal chatter might be more negative, self-defeating, and even a bit of a bully.

The inner voice is formed and influenced by both conscious and unconscious thoughts, beliefs, ideas, memories, and experiences, as well as by evolution having provided us with a brain primed to detect risk (more on this in a moment).

Take 5: Listen to Your Inner Voice

Take a few moments to reflect on how you've spoken to yourself so far today. If you're lucky, you'll have been kind and gentle. Many of us, however, often find that we aren't all that nice to ourselves, judging and criticizing ourselves a lot more than we would others.

Now consider how are you speaking to yourself in this moment—maybe even about your self-talk discoveries just now?

AN INTRODUCTION TO THINKING TRAPS

The human brain has upward of 60,000 thoughts a day—and many of these can be doubtful and discouraging.

Go easy on your mind for not spending the day in a bubble of positivity though, as negatively framed thoughts are perfectly natural and, more than that, they even serve a function (or at least they used to).

Viewing the world through a pair of rose-tinted glasses would have left cavemen and -women open to a whole host of issues back in the day. You and I may not have been around to write and read this book if our ancestors had believed in the inherent goodness of, let's say, an approaching saber-toothed tiger! You see, our brains are primed to be slightly skeptical—to be on the lookout for such threats! And it is this skepticism that has enabled our species to both survive and thrive.

The snag in the survival mechanism is that the world as we now know it has evolved at a much faster rate than our brains can keep up with, which means that our primordial instincts are still present, even now that the original threats, such as dangerous wild animals, are not.

In trying to protect us, our mind can, ironically, end up caging us in by unnecessarily amplifying the perceived risks around all sorts of situations. In psychology, these thought cages are called "thinking traps" or "cognitive distortions." In short, they are habitual errors in thinking.

Most people will find themselves in a loop of cognitive distortion from time to time. This causes a negative bias in the interpretation of events—a distortion of reality that can trigger feelings of pessimism and in some cases, depression.

But the good news is that once we recognize a cognitive distortion, it is entirely possible to do something about it.

There is a saying among neuroscientists, that: "Neurons that fire together, wire together." This means that the more a certain thought pattern occurs in your brain, the stronger and more ingrained the pattern becomes.

However, once we are able to spot a distortion in how things are "firing" and "wiring" in our brain, we have the capacity to "rewire" things and establish new patterns—in the case of negative self-talk, by speaking to ourselves in a kinder, more affirming way. In other words, with some dedication to changing our self-talk, we can eventually change the way our brain "fires."

This ability for change within the brain is known as neuroplasticity. In the same way that a scratch on our hand regenerates new tissue, the elasticity of the brain makes it possible to rewire connections of neurons to adapt helpfully under pressure.

However, only when we are willing to both recognize and address the distortions that skew our thinking, can we begin to create distance from the thoughts themselves, think more objectively, and start to instigate the change.

This may sound all very well in theory, but how can we begin to put it into practice? With a simple three-step method:

1. Notice

Identify a thought or a feeling that is creating tension within you.

2. Explore

Bring in some curiosity. Ask questions such as: What is this thought or feeling about? What function does it serve? Is this reaction historical?

3. Realign

Try to differentiate between what is thought, what is feeling, and what is true. Ask questions such as: If a loved one had this thought or feeling, what words of comfort would you offer them? Can you offer yourself the same empathetic understanding?

Don't worry if this feels a little woolly at the moment. It should start to make more sense once you see examples in action in the pages that follow—in relation to each of the types of thinking traps that we will explore.

TYPES OF THINKING TRAP

There is a range of different types of "thinking traps," or cognitive distortions, as recognized by Dr. Aaron Beck and popularized by Dr. Daniel Amen. It is worth knowing about these and looking out for them within your own thought patterns so that you can start to alter/move past/heal them. These include/are:

* Fortune-telling
* Mind-reading
* "Should"-ing
* Blaming
* Black-and-white thinking
* Emotional reasoning
* Catastrophizing
* Personalizing

Fortune-telling

We all have expectations for the future and make predictions about how we are likely to feel if these expectations do or do not come to fruition. However, the thinking trap known as "fortune-telling" involves going beyond having expectations into the realms of negative predictions. This means that when we have a thought that something bad is going to happen, we take it as fact.

The thinking trap of fortune-telling can sound like:

* "Nothing will ever work out for me"
* "I'll be alone forever"
* "I'll make a fool of myself"

Example

A romantic relationship that I've been in has come to an end.

1. *Notice*

I'm upset and the subconscious process of fortune-telling is making me think that I'm bound for a life alone. I'll never meet anyone else. Love isn't real. And the only person I can rely on is myself.

2. *Explore*

Do these seem like truths based on what has happened? Or might they be cognitive distortions? What feelings might these thoughts be attempting to shield me from? Maybe grief or loneliness? Have I worried about these things before? What are the potential benefits of believing these thoughts right now, if any?

3. **Realign**

Take a moment to breathe. What I'm experiencing right now is painful. It's difficult not to read further into this situation when the emotion I'm experiencing is so heavy. What is it that I really need right now? It's likely I need reminding of those I have around me. Can I offer this to myself in some way?

Mind-reading

"Mind-reading" is the assumption that we know what other people are thinking or will think, even though they haven't said and we haven't asked them. Certain "mind-reading" can be useful to help form connections with people such as being able to "read" the facial signals we receive from others, whether a smile, a laugh, or a jaw-drop. However, mind-reading becomes problematic when it is negative, frequent, and without much evidence to go on.

The thinking trap of mind-reading can sound like:

* "They think I'm weird"
* "They don't care about me"
* "I'm bothering them"

Example

A friend at work has become quiet and standoffish. Unbeknownst to me, this is as a result of something upsetting that has happened in their personal life.

1. **Notice**

   The subconscious process of mind-reading is making me think that my friend is behaving this way because of something I've done, and this is making me feel bad.

2. **Explore**

   Does my assumption seem like a truth based on what has happened? Or might it be a distortion? What evidence do I have to support it? Is my conclusion typical behavior of the person I know? What is it I fear might happen because of this situation?

3. **Realign**

   Let me hold the situation at arm's length. What are some other possibilities for why this has happened—ones that don't involve me? This event has given me information on a trigger I have. This is something I can do some unpacking around. Right now, what can I say to myself that is soothing? Everyone has off days, and it's rarely personal.

"Should"-ing

The word "should" is one that comes out of most of our mouths several times a day, probably without us even realizing—"I should do that ironing," "I should get that work finished," "She should learn how to drive…" But "should"-ing is actually a thinking trap that can lead us down a precarious path of judgment and criticism. And this can, in turn, lead to frustration, unhappiness, and even anger toward both ourselves and others.

Another paradoxical setback of "should"-ing is that it is actually very demotivating. Think about it. What is something you feel you "should" do right now? Does this excite you? Or make you feel apathetic? On the whole, shoulds neither get the creative juices flowing nor the productivity engine reviving.

Example

I've been procrastinating addressing certain emails in my inbox.

1. **Notice**

   As I settle down for the evening, the shoulds start piping up: "I should stop watching TV and get back to my computer," "I should respond to Andy before it gets too late," "I should get back to those other emails while I'm there."

2. **Explore**

   What concerns or fears have held me back from answering these emails before now? Perhaps, a sense of overwhelm? A fear of failure? Or maybe an underlying fear of success? How does the word "should" make me feel? Am I comfortable with this? Does it remind me of anyone, or anything, in particular?

3. **Realign**

   The shoulds are my mind's way of trying to deal with the anxiety around the task at hand. How would it sound and feel to replace "I should" with "I would like to …" or "I want to …"? It's likely I'm not giving myself enough credit and that the task could be broken down into manageable steps. Starting is always the trickiest. What small step could I take to ease the perceived weight of the task?

Blaming

Let's face it. Nobody likes admitting that they're wrong—"It wasn't my fault," "I got stuck in traffic," "I wouldn't have shouted if you hadn't made me so angry …" Unfortunately, shying away from our own accountability can often lead us to blame others, or external circumstances, for our own mistakes.

Example
I got into a shouting match with a good friend and she said something hurtful in the heat of the moment. I know it is out of character for her but, nonetheless, I feel hurt.

1. *Notice*
   Although my friend has since apologized for what she said, I still feel hurt and am continuing to focus on the many ways that I feel she was wrong. I find myself unable to apologize for the part that I played in the argument, including having raised my voice.
2. *Explore*
   Why am I continuing to focus on blame when she has said she's sorry? Does blaming my friend protect me in some way? What is it I fear about acknowl-

THINK
OF SOMEONE YOU
CARE ABOUT COMING
TO YOU WITH THE
SAME SORT OF
THOUGHTS.
WHAT WOULD YOU
TELL THEM?

edging my part in the argument? Might this be to do with how conflict was modeled at home? Or a previous experience of having my vulnerability taken advantage of?

3. *Realign*

Acknowledging the part I play in any situation doesn't eradicate another's wrongdoing; I can both feel hurt and accept responsibility for anything I have done. How would I like to handle and resolve conflict moving forward? How would that have looked in this situation? It's rational to fear being vulnerable, and yet this change is something I want for myself. What would change if I blamed others less? Is this more in keeping with how I would like to be? I can't control what my friend says, but I can control how I respond going forward.

Black-and-white Thinking

When we fall into the trap of "black-and-white thinking," also known as "polarized thinking," we think in extremes and absolutes. Everything is either fantastic or awful—"I aim for perfection, and anything less makes me a failure." Thinking in such dichotomies is the basis of perfectionism.

However, nothing exists in absolutes, so attempting to force our experience into such rigid categories can leave us feeling disappointed, disheartened, ashamed, and even hopeless. Our attempts will seldom, if ever, meet the unattainable expectations of our absolutes. Life is rarely entirely just one way or the other.

Example

I get an evaluation back at work and see that the feedback isn't as good as I'm used to getting.

1. **Notice**

   I feel completely crestfallen and this thinking trap is causing me to think I'm not cut out for the job I do. I'm not good enough and I've just been lucky up until now to even have a job.

2. **Explore**

   What evidence do I have both for and against these thoughts? What underlying belief might I have about myself that my thoughts may be stemming from and/or reinforcing? What is my relationship like with imperfection? How were achievements treated by my family as I grew up?

3. **Realign**

   Let me look at the bigger picture and remind myself of something important. This is disappointing, but marks are not a reflection of my worth. This is one piece of feedback. Why am I giving this such power? What would I say to a friend in this situation? I can feel disappointed without diminishing myself.

Emotional Reasoning

When we take our feelings as evidence of the truth, we're smack bang in the thinking trap of emotional reasoning—"I feel something, therefore my interpretation (the thoughts I'm assigning to this feeling) must be true." In reality, our feeling is valid, but our interpretation of the feeling and what ensues from this, is likely to be fairly skewed.

Example
I feel dismissed by my partner, who is constantly on their smartphone, even when I'm talking to them.

1. ***Notice***

   The subconscious process of my emotional reasoning is making me feel rejected. This, in turn, is making me think and believe that my partner doesn't care about me and is taking advantage of me.

2. ***Explore***

   Is my current thought supporting an underlying belief that I have of myself or others? Consider both the feeling and the thought separately: Have I felt like this before? And why am I putting this thought interpretation on this feeling?

3. ***Realign***

   The interpretation I've placed on my feeling may be showing me a previous wound that deserves my attention. What old message or belief am I struggling with that I wish to let go of? My feeling is valid and is my responsibility. What kind reminder can I offer myself, in light of this?

Catastrophizing

Catastrophizing is a distortion familiar to many of us. This thinking trap occurs when we take usual, run-of-the-mill situations and turn them into something horrendous and colossal. We fly straight to the worst-case scenario and the irrational. The threat has been exaggerated in our mind and we're often left feeling panicked, overwhelmed, or even hopeless.

Example
I reach for my phone in the pocket of my coat and discover it isn't there.

1. Notice
My heart starts racing and the catastrophizing thoughts start to flow. "Oh no! I've lost my phone. I've left it behind. Someone's taken it. What am I going to do? There's no way I'll be able to afford another right now. What if someone's looking at my photos this second? What if they access my passwords and hack my social media?" All of this has happened within seconds, during which I happen to spot my phone on the chair beside me!

2. Explore
Coming back to the original thought "I've lost my phone," what would make this scenario so horrendous? How would I feel about this in a week, in a month, and in a year's time? What is my relationship with control like? Might this need some attention?

3. Realign
Take a moment to breathe and slow down the thoughts. Notice what fear is present. How could I soothe this fear in this moment? What learning have I distilled from this experience? Remember, letting go of control is really just letting go of the illusion of control.

Personalizing

"Personalization" is one of the most common thinking traps. This can involve taking things too much to heart (too "personally"); blaming yourself for circumstances that aren't connected to you or that are beyond your control; and incorrectly assuming that you've been targeted or left out from things on purpose.

Being willing to take accountability for our choices is, of course, a great indicator of self-development and emotional intelligence, but at the same time holding yourself responsible for things that aren't your fault is very unhelpful, particularly if you end up feeling like a victim of circumstance.

Example

I receive the end-of-year report from my daughter's school, only to find out that she's struggling in math.

1. **Notice**

   The subconscious process of personalization tells me that this is all my fault. I should have picked up on it, or inquired into it, sooner. I'm a bad parent.

2. **Explore**

   What part have I realistically played in the outcome and how might I not be entirely to blame? Does blame have to exist in this situation at all? What is the purpose of personalizing this? Does it protect me or anyone else from something? Does it help at all?

3. *Realign*

Take a step back from the situation. What is it that needs to be done? Things like this happen. There doesn't have to be blame and fault, but understanding this thinking trap pattern is useful for me going forward. What would I say to a friend if they felt this way? There is no room for "perfection" in any given situation, including parenting.

Thinking Traps Summary

Having read all the information on the various thinking traps, you'll hopefully now have a richer understanding of not only the thinking traps themselves, but also the sense of increased ease and calm that can be created through starting to notice, explore, and realign these in your life. Always feel free to tailor your exploration and realignment processes to best work with your personal needs and experiences, and just see what insights you come to.

RECOGNIZING OUR INNER BULLY

Unfortunately, many of us often speak to ourselves in the voice of a bully rather than in a kind, supportive way. Sometimes the inner bully battens down the hatches and makes such a home within our minds that we're not even aware of its presence until a friend or a therapist points out that we're being too hard on ourselves. In fact, it's not uncommon for our inner bully to become so powerful that it starts to have detrimental effects on our well-being.

The "greatest hits" (or most common comments) of the inner bully can sound something like:

"You look awful"

"That was the dumbest thing you've ever done"

"Everyone else has their life in order, except you"

"Why bother? You won't be any good!"

"You have nothing good to say"

"You're embarrassing yourself"

Take 5: Know Your Playlist

If the idea of the inner bully having a "greatest hits" album that it plays on repeat is something that resonates with you, take a moment to reflect on what your inner bully's "greatest hits" are. And consider how you would like to change these.

GETTING TO KNOW OUR INNER BULLY

As many of us know, it can be really difficult to speak to ourselves with gentleness and softness. The idea of doing so might make us cringe or it might elicit feelings of frustration and anger when we're unable to speak kindly to ourselves or can't see the point in it. When we have a low sense of selfhood, we can become more comfortable with the bully voice emerging than sitting with what lies beneath; the bully is familiar, whereas the exploration of our fears is not.

Our brain is wired to distance us from fear, and to lean into what's certain and familiar, even if this inadvertently moves us away from our sense of self. Our inner bully's function then is often to keep us distracted from looking at any subconscious fears that may have been activated in us.

At other times, the voice of the inner bully is likely to reiterate messages that we've internalized from an outer voice in our childhood—a scathing voice that we've heard so much from over the years that they've become woven into the fabric of ourselves. This voice might be that of a critical caregiver who had unrealistic expectations of us when we were young. Early trauma, such as bullying and other forms of abuse, can also play an integral role in the way we speak to ourselves.

At the core of the inner bully is a deep sense of shame. Shame doesn't say, "I've done something wrong." Shame says, "I am wrong." Anything that diminishes our spirit has the potential to erode our sense of self.

THE INNER BULLY
IS JUST ONE PART
OF YOU, AT YOUR INNER
CONFERENCE MEETING,
HOGGING THE MIC.

ISN'T IT TIME WE TURNED
OUR ATTENTION TO THE
OTHER PARTS OF YOU AT
THE TABLE?

HEALING OUR SELF-TALK

In the pages that follow we'll look at ways we can heal our self-talk through a six-step process, particularly when the inner bully is mouthing off:

1. Inspect your self-talk
2. Explore the purpose of your self-talk
3. Address your resistance to compassion
4. Parent the bully
5. Practice self-affirmation
6. Reflect

Take 5: Observe the Bully

Before starting the six-step process outlined above, take a moment to note that the inner bully isn't you. It may be a part of you but it is not all of you. You're the one who overhears and *spots* the bully. You're the one who has the power to acknowledge and speak back to it when it appears.

When the bully emerges, try holding it at arm's length to maintain some distance from it, then listen with an impassive ear. Feel into how this changes the dynamic of your relation with it, and how you subsequently feel.

1. Inspect Your Self-Talk

Take time to observe how you speak to yourself. What words are you using? What tone does your self-talk speak in? Remember that when your sense of self is low, self-talk tends to sound more critical and bully-like than normal. So does the way you're speaking to yourself change depending on your environment? What about the time of day or year? Or the people you're spending time with? Does the voice remind you of anyone? What about the words themselves? Are they yours? Or do they sound more like someone else you know? Gently explore the content of your self-talk and consider how you could rework each negative thought that comes up through a lens of increased tolerance and compassion.

2. Explore the Purpose of Your Self-Talk

As mentioned earlier, there are always reasons for us speaking to ourselves in the manner we do; the inner bully has a purpose to serve. Sometimes, this is to protect us from an emotion that we fear will be overwhelming. Sometimes it might be to stop us from doing something that would make us feel vulnerable. Sometimes it may be due to a fear of failure or a fear of success. Negative self-talk can also serve to keep us in a place of familiar "victimhood"; if we're a victim of circumstance, we can deny responsibility for our own well-being. This isn't something to judge yourself for. What we believe of ourselves, we'll find evidence for. It takes resilience and courage to acknowledge it.

So explore and feel into these options around why you feel your bully talks to you in the way it does—and, indeed, why you allow it to do so. And, of course, seek the help of a therapist or other mental health professional if ever you need support. As you continue to discover the function of your self-talk, you will increasingly discover opportunities to heal.

3. Address Your Resistance to Compassion

Speaking to yourself with gentleness, tolerance, and compassion may seem like a feat of Everest proportions. We may be quick to roll our eyes at the idea or we might have wanted to skip this section entirely as it feels too "wishy-washy" and New Agey, or maybe even just too challenging and uncomfortable.

Many resist the idea of compassion due to it being such an overused buzzword of late. But it's important not to dismiss its inherent value just because of the over-utilization of it as a group of letters.

As we learn to speak to ourselves in a way that is more compassionate, understanding, and comforting, it is likely to highlight the absence of this type of kindness to ourselves up until this point. There is a grief in noticing how we've spoken to ourselves in the past. But in each new way of speaking to ourselves lies the potential for a new way of being.

Healing is active work. Although words like compassion, tolerance, patience, acceptance, and gentleness indicate softness, the work toward becoming each of these things is anything but easy.

4. Parent the Bully

A lesson we usually learn in childhood: If anyone is bullying either you or someone you know, inform a parent or a teacher. This lesson doesn't change in adulthood, the only difference being that the bully, the parent, and the teacher all now lie within.

The inner bully is well established at making us feel "less than," so it makes sense to deliberately bring in the voice of our supportive inner parent or teacher to counteract this.

So, what would your inner parent say to your inner bully? Perhaps they would be firm and assertive? Maybe they're concerned for the bully, wondering what has happened to make them speak the way they do? Might they have questions for them? Can they see through the exterior of the bully to what's really going on beneath the meanness?

The inner parent, something we will explore further in Chapter 7, may be currently unfamiliar to you but they're more than ready to step in, protect, and restore safety. So try to bring conscious attention to what your inner parent is feeling when the bully next starts speaking.

5. Practice Self-Affirmation

When we see the word affirmation, we might think of awkwardly muttering a string of positive statements to ourselves in the mirror.

An affirmation is actually any positive statement that we repeatedly say to ourselves. It can be as simple as "I am happy" or "I am smart."

Our conscious mind is good at thinking rationally and systematically about what it is we say to ourselves, but our subconscious mind cannot do this. It accepts our inner dialogue as truth, which is why developing a practice of regular, conscious self-affirmation is invaluable to our sense of self. It's important to remember that belief comes with time, so commitment and consistency are vital.

See the pages that follow for further insight into affirmations, including a list of affirmations to choose from and guidance on creating your own.

6. Reflect

As we become active in healing our self-talk, it's important that we take time to reflect on the ways we've spoken to ourselves since our last check-in. So how did you speak to yourself today? How active was the inner bully today? Did you forget to call on the voice of your inner parent?

By bringing daily conscious attention to the ways we speak to ourselves and continually recommitting to parenting ourselves with compassion, we amplify our healing.

There is no room for perfection in this process. We're presented with new opportunities to learn about ourselves every day. So the trick is to stay curious, keep going, and keep reflecting.

AFFIRMATIONS FOR SKEPTICS

Some might find the idea of affirmations a bit "woo-woo," and I understand that. But please know that the value of developing a conscious affirmation practice has been repeatedly supported through both neuroscientific and empirical research.

I can still feel a little skeptical when starting afresh with a new affirmation practice. So whether you're experiencing this skepticism with me, or you're excited and raring to go, all I ask is that you read the information that follows with an open heart and an open mind.

As briefly mentioned earlier, affirmations are short, positive statements that, when repeated regularly, filter through the conscious mind into the subconscious. Used effectively, they can enable us to positively influence our thought patterns, our behavior, and how we feel about ourselves.

Research shows that affirmation practice is linked with better sleep, personal achievement, reduced defensiveness, lower stress levels, and an improved perspective of the self. So understandably, there's significant hype around the practice. The main issue with positive affirmations is they can feel uncomfortably positive. So, let's remove the pressure of positivity, and begin with neutrality.

KEY AFFIRMATION INGREDIENTS

There are three essential elements for every affirmation recipe, without which the brain cannot process the statement with ease. These ensure the effectiveness of your practice and cut out any extra work the mind would have to do. They are:

* ***The Present Tense:***

Affirmations need to be statements based in the present, not the future—so, for example, "I feel good about myself" (not "I will feel good about myself").

This is because our subconscious mind cannot differentiate between what is past, future, and present; it needs specifics. Statements such as "I want to be happy" or "I will feel more energetic" would introduce uncertainty and ambiguity. *Want* to be happy? *Will* feel more energetic? *When!? Let's put that off because that sounds like effort!* If you write a story with too many plot holes, the subconscious finishes the script!

* ***Neutrality:***

Each statement should only include affirming words. Our brains have to work overtime to extract the good from affirmations that contain words like "won't" or "can't."

Therefore avoid phrasings such as "I won't criticize myself" and instead try something like "I'm OK. I am working on accepting myself for the good human I am."

* ***Definitive Content:***

All affirmations need to be spoken as definitive truths. As such, be mindful not to include words like "if," "might," "should," "could," or "I'll try…."

Therefore avoid phrasings such as "If something good happens to me, I'll try not to write it off as a stroke of luck," and instead try something along the lines of "I am deserving of all the good that is coming into my life" or "Good things happen and I'm accepting that I play a part in that."

An interesting observation:

If you come across an affirmation that makes you squirm, it's more than likely a statement that you really need right now, whether you like it or not—so give it a go. Sometimes, what we resist the most, we're most in need of. As mentioned earlier, you don't need to believe in the affirmation to start with and it doesn't need to be reflective of your life as it is in this moment.

Take 5: Take Your Affirmation Meds

1 affirmation
Spoken aloud 2x daily
For 30+ days

MANAGING OUR AFFIRMATION EXPECTATIONS

An affirmation practice understandably takes, well, *practice*, but that doesn't mean you have to wait a really long time for change to occur. Depending on what you're working on, you may start noticing changes in the third week or even on the first day. It will be completely different for each individual.

The brain has, up until now, simply been enjoying what is familiar, even if the familiar has been a thought pattern that has been chipping away at our self-esteem.

Familiarity is simply a strong neural pathway in the brain. So for change to occur, we need to form *new* roadmaps in the brain. And this is why repetition is crucial, as is speaking each affirmation aloud.

You're literally mapping a new way of being, so stay consistent and let your voice be heard.

Realigning thoughts (and ways of being) is hard but exciting work. Be patient with yourself. As you become consistent with your practice, you will begin to notice your chosen affirmation(s) resonating deeper.

Take 5: Choose a Daily Affirmation

Firstly, identify a thought you would like to leave behind. Next, choose an affirmation that is in alignment with where you wish to be; you can either choose one from the list below or look elsewhere for inspiration. Repeat the chosen affirmation daily.

AFFIRMATIONS TO CHOOSE FROM

* My mind is calm
* I have value and I matter
* I feel the joy of abundance

* I feel good today
* I am on my right path
* I find healing within me daily
* I am content
* I am healthy and healing
* I deserve this
* My life is filled with love
* I am whole as I am
* I am growing

Take 5: Write Your Own Affirmation

If you'd rather create your own affirmation based on everything you've been exploring about yourself so far, then use the three key ingredients explained on page 113, and see how working with your personalized affirmation each day makes you feel.

SELF-TALK FIRST AID KIT

Even when our life generally looks and feels like it's in a good place, we all experience difficult days, and difficult moments. At such times, words of reassurance from others can be an indispensable source of comfort.

AN AFFIRMATION
PRACTICE IS
IMPORTANT.
IT'S ALSO IMPORTANT
TO CONSIDER
HOW CAN I LIVE
THIS AFFIRMATION?

However, other people are not always readily available to offer such reassurance, so see below for some gentle, supportive reminders that you can give yourself any time you need them.

Reassurance For Anxious Moments

* In this moment, I'm experiencing feelings I don't like, but that's OK. It will pass, just like it arrived.
* If I feel anxious, I feel anxious—so what!? It's a part of life, but it's not bigger than life.
* I've had anxious moments before, and I made it through all of them. I'm going to breathe in for 3. Hold for 3. And exhale for 3.
* What I'm feeling is difficult, but it isn't static. It moves. And it will move on.
* This is uncomfortable but it isn't dangerous; it's data. I'm going to focus on my breath right now and get curious about what it's trying to tell me.
* Anxiety is a rational feeling attempting to communicate with me in an irrational way.
* Each time I accept that I'm having an anxious moment I grow my capacity to cope with it.

Reassurance For Tough Days

* I don't need to rush. I can take things slowly.
* I've felt like this before, so I know I can handle it.

* A bad day doesn't mean I'm bad or that my life is bad.
* One low day doesn't take away the many days that have felt good. Even today there have been moments that have felt lighter.
* In this moment, it's hard to believe I will feel better, but I also know on some level that I will.
* This feeling isn't every part of me. I'm feeling low, but it's one piece of what I'm feeling.
* It's OK if today isn't going, or hasn't gone, to plan.
* It takes courage and resilience to acknowledge that I'm feeling challenged, and here I am, doing just that.

Reassurance When Anger Appears

* Feeling angry is healthy and I'm responsible for how I manage it.
* Anger is an emotion that I'm comfortable with. What else am I feeling that isn't so comfortable for me?
* I can allow this feeling to be here and to process through my body.
* I can take some time and breathe until I know what it is I would like to do.
* Anger is a valuable ally, but aggression is not. I can communicate my anger in a calm manner when I feel ready.
* It doesn't feel like it right now, but the depth of my anger will subside soon.
* I am safe. I am safe. I am safe.

MENTAL NOTES

Take five minutes at the end of each day for a month to reflect on the following:

* How would I like to speak to myself tomorrow? For example, I might like to be kinder, more patient, and/or more encouraging.

* What will my newly enhanced self-talk sound like? For example, instead of berating myself for anything that goes off track, I might say things like "I'm really enjoying this project" and "It's OK to make mistakes."

* What new affirmation can I write to support this? For example, "I am enough," "I am creative," "I am loved ..."

After the month, you'll have an abundance of knowledge about how you treat yourself and talk to yourself, including actionable steps in terms of how you will be kinder to yourself in the future.

4.
Recognizing Triggers

HOW TO UNDERSTAND YOUR REACTIONS

"We meet ourselves time and again in a thousand disguises on the path of life."
Carl Jung

So, what do we mean by the term "triggers?" Triggers are emotional buttons. They connect the present moment into a memory or situation in the past that was painful or traumatic for us. This can happen either consciously or unconsciously, and can be felt both emotionally and physically.

Although triggers are often associated with severe conditions like PTSD (Post Traumatic Stress Disorder), they are very common so can also be the result of more minor negative associations with certain places, people, or events.

WHY GET TO KNOW OUR TRIGGERS?

Learning about our triggers goes hand in hand with learning about who we are. Getting to know our triggers is an important step in the wider journey of self-understanding as it makes us more self-aware.

When we're more self-aware, it is possible to mitigate our reactions and manage our emotions, rather than losing our sense of self and letting them control us. Being aware also helps us to know where the parameters are on what we're able to tolerate. We can then choose to limit our exposure to our triggers while we work through the emotional charge at the root of them.

Noting and identifying our triggers can also alert us to the state of our own mental health and wellbeing, shining a light on any old emotional wounds that require attention.

However, working with our triggers can make us feel anxious, panicked, overwhelmed, or sad. In more severe cases, we can also experience flashbacks, causing us to lose track of the here and now and relive the trauma as if it were in the present. Strong reactions to triggers like this are best addressed with the support of a trauma therapist or your doctor.

Take 5: Identify a Trigger for You

Can you recall a situation in which you felt "triggered?"

How did it make you feel? Perhaps your thoughts raced and your heart pounded? Perhaps your mind filled with white noise and you felt an urgency to escape? At other times, we can go into what is known as autopilot. When this happens, we may say things that we wouldn't normally say; so might this be something you recognize?

DIFFERENT TYPES OF TRIGGERS

Triggers can occur both internally and externally. Internal triggers are bodily sensations that we connect to similar feelings we had at the time, such as a racing heart or stomach pain. External triggers include stimuli outside us such as the sound of someone shouting, a particular smell, a particular type of touch, financial issues, and a wide range of other things. See the image on the next page for some more examples of both internal and external triggers.

A trigger is usually specific to an individual. But it need not be closely related to the experience of the original event. Even when a person encounters the same stimuli in another context (which the thinking brain can rationalize), the survival brain associates the triggers with the original trauma or situation. For instance, things like the

INTERNAL TRIGGERS	EXTERNAL TRIGGERS
A PHYSICAL SENSATION	ANNIVERSARIES + SIGNIFICANT DATES
HIGH LEVELS OF STRESS + ANXIETY	THE NEWS
	FINANCIAL ISSUES
FEELING RIDICULED + UNHEARD	LOUD NOISES
ROUTINES	WITNESSING CONFLICT + VIOLENCE

anniversary date of a trauma, a loud noise, financial stress, or family friction can cause the survival brain to recall and relive the original wound.

Sometimes triggers are a feeling, rather than an event. For example, we could experience a level of tension or powerlessness that was omnipresent in childhood; or when someone ignores our voice, we may feel taken for granted or unloved. These emotional buttons are often pushed when in conflict with our partner or someone within our close social circle.

A renowned relationship research body called The Gottman Institute compiled a list of 24 common triggers that are often activated in conflict with other people.

As you read these, see if any of them particularly resonate with you:

1. I felt excluded

2. I felt powerless

3. I felt unheard

4. I felt scolded

5. I felt judged

6. I felt blamed

7. I felt disrespected

8. I felt a lack of affection

9. I felt uncared for

10. I felt lonely

11. I felt ignored

12. I felt like I couldn't be honest

13. I felt like the bad guy

14. I felt forgotten

15. I felt unsafe

16. I felt unloved

17. I felt like that was unfair

18. I felt frustrated

19. I felt disconnected

20. I felt trapped

21. I felt a lack of passion

22. I felt like I couldn't speak up

23. I felt manipulated

24. I felt controlled

UNDERSTANDING TRIGGERING

It's easier to forgive the actions of both ourselves and others when we realize the strength of the connections between our environment, our emotions, and our reactions—and that emotional triggering is, in fact, a survival response.

However, knowing about our triggers doesn't give us free rein to do whatever we wish, of course. Triggers explain; they don't excuse. Just as learning about our attachment style helps us to understand our relationships, learning about triggers helps us to understand our reactions and recognize situations that might activate them.

This gives us the opportunity to move from a place of unconscious, knee-jerk reactions to conscious, considered responses. And it empowers us to cope better when we find ourselves in situations where our emotional buttons are being pushed.

When we begin to understand our triggers, and the various ways they affect us all, we can begin to take all the energy we may have previously put into berating ourselves and channel it into change instead.

Note to self:

1. If you're human, you'll have triggers.
2. If you're human, there's not another person alive who won't trigger you.

LEARNING TO RECOGNIZE YOUR TRIGGERS

The next time you feel that you have been triggered by a particular situation, event, or person, try to take a breath and step back from it a little so that, instead of getting completely wrapped up in it, you can try the following five-step process. You can do this process anywhere safe and comfortable, and it should only take you between five and ten minutes.

1. Notice Your Body

Pay attention to how your body feels when you feel you've been triggered and take a mental note of its reactions. Have your muscles tensed? How is your temperature? Is your face hot? Are your hands cold? How deeply are you breathing? Take stock of your body's responses, however subtle or extreme they may be.

2. Observe Your Thoughts

Now turn your focus to your thoughts. What stories are present? Use the information on Thinking Traps in Chapter 3 to check which of these "cognitive distortions" might be present? You don't have to do anything with this information right now. Your only job is to notice what thoughts appear, without changing or reacting to them. Try jotting some of these thoughts down on paper, in your journal, or in your phone.

3. Don Your Detective Hat

It's now time to put on your deerstalker and channel your inner Sherlock. Start to get curious about the situation that has activated both these physical and emotional responses within you. It may not be so obvious at first but take time to consider the possibilities. Look back at the information earlier in this chapter to help guide your investigation. Perhaps the trigger was a word, or a tone of voice? Maybe it was a smell? Or an overriding feeling? Or maybe it was an opinion that someone shared or a situation that in some way reflected back a negative belief you have about yourself?

It is often the case that many of our triggers (because we all have many) amalgamate. For example, your trigger in a particular moment could be a combination of a loud crowd, your uncomfortable jumper, the workload waiting for you at home, the two blue ticks on an unanswered WhatsApp message, *and* an underlying belief that you're treated unfairly in relationships. We all have a host of triggers that we're unaware of and that we can only recognize after we've been activated.

4. Identify Unmet Needs

Take some time to reflect on whether you feel the trigger you've just experienced might be connected to any unmet needs or wishes in your life, such as safety, reliability, attention, or affection? If so, consider how this need, or wish, was treated by the people you've been in relationships with throughout your life, whether family, friends, partners, or whoever else?

It's perfectly normal for some needs to go unmet into adult life. It would be impossible, and perhaps unwise, for others to meet every need we have with consistency and alacrity. Yet, when a need is consistently unmet or disregarded throughout our life, an emotional wound of some sort usually develops which can emerge in all sorts of ways, including as a potential trigger.

Looking back on our life so far with hindsight and maturity, we may now be able to understand *why* certain needs in our life weren't met. A caregiver may, for example, have been doing the very best they could but simply not have had as much time and energy as they wanted as they also had to work full-time to put food on the table. Likewise, in past relationships, whether with friends or romantic partners, we may have felt disrespected or taken for granted but understood that the other person was going through something difficult at the time. Although this helps us to understand what happened, it doesn't take away from the emotional wound, and the associated experience of disappointment and/or pain.

5. Take a Wider View

Finally, consider what day-to-day factors may have contributed to the extent of the trigger; as, let's face it, there are many things that can contribute to us feeling tetchy, sensitive, or on edge on any given day. Perhaps, there's none today, but it's equally possible that we slept poorly, we skipped lunch, or we had to spend time in a crowded, noisy supermarket earlier that day. There are any number of factors that can contribute to what we are able to cope with. When you start ascertaining what these influences are, you can better care for your emotional well-being by taking moments throughout the day to check in with how you're feeling and what you might need.

The more you focus on identifying and working through any issues that trigger you, the less likely you'll be to "act out" based on the emotions that bubble to the surface. You might sense a trigger's presence, but as you unpack the situation through reflection and realignment, you should start to notice how the emotional charge attached to the situation begins to dull and dissolve. As you grow more practiced in spotting and working with your triggers, the circumstances that once knocked you off-kilter will gradually lose their charge and, subsequently, their control.

HEALING OUR TRIGGERS

Working through triggers will look different for everybody. With that in mind, below are some steps to take that may help us begin to lessen the emotional charge of triggers and start the process of healing.

WHY AM I FEELING THIS WAY? STOP BEING SO STUPID!
THERE IS LIKELY A GOOD EXPLANATION FOR WHY I FEEL THIS WAY, EVEN IF I DON'T KNOW WHAT THAT IS YET

Please note that while it is possible to work through this process on your own (potentially with the help of a journal if you like working this way), some people may prefer to do this kind of work with the support of a qualified therapist, particularly in instances of trauma.

The first step in healing a trigger is being conscious of it, which the steps already outlined above offer you help with.

The next step is to find somewhere you feel safe and comfortable. Safety is integral. We cannot heal in a space that we don't feel safe in. It is very difficult, and at times risky, to begin deeper work when in an unsure environment, whereas a calm, secure place (whatever that looks like for you) will provide the kind of holding that you need for healing.

You can now start to compassionately explore how you feel in your body when this trigger crops up. For example, you might feel dizzy, nauseous, or tense.

Next, start considering any beliefs connected with the trigger in hand. You may, for example, find that you're carrying with you a set of theories, or "stories," about yourself from previous relationships or early childhood experiences that are doing more harm than good, such as "I'm stupid" or "I'm too emotional." Gently consider these parts of you that feel "less than" and begin to speak to yourself about them with the kindness and compassion you would offer a loved one. What you'll notice over time is that when you begin to work on one area, the results and rewards start to trickle into *all* aspects of who you are.

Lessening the emotional charge of triggers also involves tracing their origin. So, again, get curious about where they may have originated. For instance, if we notice ourselves becoming defensive over something that's been said to us, why might this be? Perhaps it sounded like something a parent or a teacher has said to us in the past? Maybe the tone of voice reminded us of someone in particular? Where might this type of reaction have been needed previously? The goal isn't to necessarily relive the event, nor is it to escape uncomfortable emotion. You're aiming for a healthy middle ground: recalling while staying firmly rooted in the present. Tracing a trigger within safe parameters in this way allows us to feel the emotion in a safe, grounded way, provides us with a better understanding of who we are, and teaches us why we react in particular ways.

From there, with practice, we can begin to choose how we wish to respond to our triggers, rather than having knee-jerk reactions from historic wounds.

Entering a state of increased clarity and balance enhances our ability to respond consciously to a triggering event. We can move toward such a state of balance by developing our self-regulation techniques, which we will explore in the next chapter. It's important to note that when we've experienced trauma, sensory and bodywork regulation of this nature can sometimes feel overwhelming and take us beyond what we're capable of tolerating. In such instances, it's important to reach out to a qualified trauma practitioner.

Remember: Managing and healing triggers takes time, practice, and compassionate patience. So be gentle with yourself.

Take 5: Question Your Triggers

When triggered, it may be useful to ask yourself:

* Am I reacting to what is happening in this moment, or am I reacting to something in the past?
* Am I reacting to what is happening or what I fear will happen?
* Am I reacting to what has been said or a story that I've attached to what has been said?
* What boundary, if any, has been crossed?
* What do I need in this moment?
* How can I practice self-care in this moment? (E.g., taking ten minutes out, deep breathing, calling a friend, journaling, reinstating boundaries…)

UNDERSTANDING DIFFERENT STRESS RESPONSES

In order to understand the process of triggering a little better, it is useful to understand how stress responses work in our body.

During a painful event or experience of trauma, the brain will often etch sensory stimuli into our memory; sensory information such as sights, sounds, and smells play a big role in our unconscious memories. The more sensory information is stored there, the easier a memory is to recollect. Sometimes, a sensory trigger can therefore cause an emotional reaction within you before you even realize what, why, or where these emotions have come from.

When a person is in a threatening situation, the body goes on high alert, prioritizing its reserves to react to the situation at hand. Functions that aren't essential for survival, such as digestion and the formation of short-term memory, are "switched off." And in the case of a traumatic event, a person's brain may even misfile the memory, so that instead of being stored as a past event, the situation might be labeled as an ongoing threat. When a person is then reminded of a past trauma by a "trigger," their body can sometimes act as if the event is happening again in the moment.

When the fear center of the brain, called the amygdala, detects threat, it sends an alarm call of messages through the body and brain. Our brains therefore become wired to respond to our triggers, sidestepping rational thought and going straight into one of a number of survival responses.

These can be categorized as:

* Fight Response
* Flight Response
* Freeze Response
* Fawn Response

The stress response can be essential for our survival as it motivates actions where the aim is to keep or create distance from further threat and it can indicate to those in our environment that what we're dealing with is stressful and we need some support. As you read through each section below, see which of the stress responses are most familiar to you.

Fight Response

We're likely to experience a fight response when we perceive a threat that we believe we can conquer. Our brain quickly sends messages to our body to prepare it for a physical altercation.

The characteristics of the "fight response" can include:

* Crying
* An intense feeling of anger or rage
* A feeling of wanting to hurt someone, or yourself
* Verbally or physically attacking the source of danger
* A desire to stomp the feet or kick out
* Clenching the jaw and grinding the teeth
* A burning, knotted sensation in the stomach
* A feeling of "fight" in your gaze and in your words and tone

Flight Response

If we're met by a threat or danger, whether real or perceived, the brain will prepare the body to run away when it believes that this is the most efficient way to escape it.

The characteristics of the "flight response" can include:

* Feeling restless, trapped, and tense
* Fidgeting and bouncing legs

* Constantly moving your extremities
* Excessive exercise
* Dilated and darting eyes
* Heightened anxiety
* Shallow breathing

Freeze Response

We enter into freeze mode when both mind and body feel that neither fighting (fight response) nor running (flight response) are a wise choice, or indeed a choice at all.

The characteristics of the "freeze response" can include:

* Feeling rigid, heavy, or stuck in some part of the body
* Feeling cold and/or numbness in the body
* Holding the breath or shallow breathing
* A sense of dread
* Decreased heart rate
* Skin going pale

Fawn Response

When our systems have tried the fight, flight, and freeze responses many times over without the desired result, we can fall into the often lesser known stress response called "fawn mode." Individuals who default into this have often been exposed to some kind of ongoing traumatic situations in their past. According to Patrick Walden, the pioneering researcher behind this stress response, the fawn response is best summarized as a form of people-pleasing.

Some of the characteristics of the "fawn response" include:

* Avoiding conflict
* Having a hard time saying "no"
* Taking care of others to the detriment of own wellbeing
* Self-censoring
* Feeling resentful and taken advantage of
* Social anxiety and worrying about fitting in
* Low sense of self-worth
* Fear of expressing needs and being viewed as "a burden"

Like all the other responses, this is a form of self-protection. It has helped, and continues to help, those subjected to trauma to make it through abusive situations by assuaging stress and making them feel safer in the moment. However, it also increases the likelihood of them censoring their own thoughts and emotions, preventing them from healing or seeking support from caring people in the longer term.

THE PURPOSE OF EACH STRESS RESPONSE

If there was a strong sense of love and security in your childhood, chances are that you will have access to all four of the stress responses just outlined. As each response is useful, different ones will emerge depending on the situation we find ourselves in:

* The fight response is mainly about self-protection, although it doesn't necessarily mean "ready for a fight"; it can also be about general assertiveness and expressing/holding firm boundaries.
* The flight response generally occurs in an untraumatized individual when conflict would place them in danger.
* The same individual might experience the freeze response if further effort (whether fighting or fleeing) would be viewed as wasted energy or ineffectual.
* Lastly, an untraumatized individual would sense that fawn mode could be useful if assisting, negotiating, and listening to the viewpoint of others seems like it could be the most effective way of dialing down the emotional temperature of a situation.

However, when a person has been subjected to experience of trauma, they may rely heavily on, or get "stuck" in, one main mode of functioning—making this become a default response. This limits them from accessing other modes apt to the situation at hand, and it serves to keep them distracted from uncomfortable emotions beneath the surface of their chosen defense.

The good news is that once you understand your default stress response, it enables you to recognize it going forward and from there, you have the opportunity to learn more about what measures and coping skills you may need to add to your repertoire.

YOUR BODY
HAS THE VERY
BEST OF INTENTIONS,
EVEN WHEN ITS
REACTIONS SEEM
DISPROPORTIONATE
OR SLIGHTLY
SKEWED

As with attachment, there isn't any one response to stress that is necessarily better or worse than the others. However, we may inflict more damage to ourselves if we get stuck in one mode, make an error of judgment, or perceive threats that aren't real.

Once you can identify which stress response (or stress mode) you tend to use most, the next step is to know what works for you when you are starting to feel triggered in this way. How can you calm yourself? What do you find is helpful in managing difficult emotions? The goal here is not to avoid or hide feelings but to acknowledge what is there, without shame or frustration. An emotion is just an emotion. It has no moral attachment. Feeling jealous, angry, or "needy" doesn't make you a bad person. It makes you human. We tend to suffer from our emotions when we try to avoid them or pretend they're not there, and when we ridicule and judge ourselves for their very presence.

So simply acknowledging a feeling is a big step. But where do we go from there? From there, we can begin to address how to soothe and regulate ourselves as addressed in the next chapter.

UNDERSTANDING OUR "WINDOW OF TOLERANCE"

We all do our best to handle the anxiety and stress that appears in our day-to-day lives—until we simply can't anymore. After all, everyone has a limit.

It has happened to us all—the moment that we reach what feels like a point of no return. In these moments, our rational and regulated minds and bodies give way to shouting, storming off, shutting down—whether we're with a partner, friends, siblings, parents, or whoever else. In these moments, we're no longer able to manage what's going on in our inner world. We've gone beyond the threshold of our "window of tolerance."

The window of tolerance, a term coined by Dr. Dan Siegel in 1999, describes the zone in which a person is best able to function. When we're within our window of tolerance, we are able to listen, process, reflect, integrate, rationalize, and respond to the demands of everyday life without much difficulty. Within this window, our mind and body function well, and we have the capacity to process what comes our way without being blown off course.

When we're outside of our window of tolerance, on the other hand—whether due to one main trigger or an accumulation of smaller stressors—the body responds by activating our fight, flight, freeze, or fawn modes.

Both the fight and flight responses can be categorized as states of "hyperarousal," while both the freeze and fawn responses can be categorized as states of "hypo-arousal."

Hyperarousal

In hyperarousal, we're alert and ready to react. This tends to show itself externally, for example through behavior like crying, shouting, stomping our feet, clenching fists, or wanting to lash out.

Signs of hyperarousal (fight or flight):

* Anxiety
* Anger or aggression

* Emotional outbursts
* Reactivity
* Overwhelm
* Impulsivity
* Controlling behavior
* Obsessive-compulsive behavior or thoughts
* Addictions
* Disordered eating

Hypo-arousal

In hypo-arousal, we tend to withdraw and shut down. This might manifest itself by feeling the need to stay in bed all day or disconnect from those around us. Hypo-arousal can be a default reaction for some, but it can also occur when we have stayed too long in hyperarousal, causing the brain and body's reaction abilities to plummet.

Signs of hypo-arousal (freeze or fawn):

* Memory loss
* Being withdrawn and/or isolating
* Dissociation
* Depression
* Lethargy
* Emptiness
* Apathy

* Being on "autopilot"
* Flat expression
* Disorientation

What Size Is Our Window of Tolerance?

It's pretty clear then that we're able to cope best with daily stressors and triggers when we operate within our window of tolerance, rather than falling into either of the states on either side.

However, a traumatic experience or unmet childhood needs can narrow our window, lessening our capacity to go along with the ebb and flow of life and to cope without getting overwhelmed.

Can you think of someone who has an unruffled and (perhaps irritatingly) grounded demeanor? If so, they most likely have a wide window of tolerance, which basically means that, although they experience anxiety, anger, and sadness like all the rest of us, they can generally do so without feeling overwhelmed or overburdened.

On the other hand, something that might appear minor to you could tip another person over the edge of their threshold. To you, their reaction may seem disproportionate to the situation at hand. But behind the scenes it makes sense as they have reached their tipping point.

It might be helpful to consider the window of tolerance like a coffee cup: the more hot water you pour in, the closer the coffee comes to the surface of the mug. The higher the level of coffee in the mug, the less water you need for the coffee to spill over entirely.

Affected by our environment, our relationship with our window of tolerance can change at different points in our life. People are, for example, typically more able to stay within their window of tolerance when they feel well supported. At certain points, you may have a greater capacity to cope with stress but feel particularly susceptible to the sadness of people who are feeling low. While at other times, you may feel fine about sitting with the sadness of others, yet flinch at the sound of a raised voice. What your window looks like today will inevitably change and grow as you continue your journey of self-understanding.

Take 5: Check in with Your Window

Take a moment to note your current level of: (i) anxiety, (ii) stress, and (iii) happiness.

* What factors increase each emotion the most? Make a list.
* Where are you within your window of tolerance right now?
* What cues might you be able to notice when you're reaching the edge of your window? Both verbal and non-verbal?

WIDENING THE WINDOW OF TOLERANCE

Learning where you stand at any given point in relation to your window of tolerance is an important step toward self-understanding. Identifying where you are will help toward the next part of the therapeutic process in this book: implementing techniques that will help to restore a sense of calm and safety within you. And implementing these practices will, in turn, help to widen your window.

Widening the window won't stop experiences of things like stress, anxiety, and sadness, unfortunately. What it will do, however, is expand our capacity to cope with what life throws at us so that, rather than feeling at the mercy of our emotions, we can approach stimuli and triggers in a way that we want to (which is great for knocking the "I should have said this!" rhetoric on the head). If we're to think back to our coffee cup example, the mug gets bigger!

Note to self: It's wise to practice new coping mechanisms as detailed in the next chapter on the good days, when you're not feeling overwhelmed or disconnected. That way when you are having a difficult moment or a hard day, you've already laid the foundations. And you've already built your capacity to access practices that help bring you a sense of calm and connection.

Not all of the self-regulation practices will be for you, but that's OK. Find the ones that appeal to you and leave the others. The more regularly you practice the ones you choose, the greater capacity you will have to understand your reactions and to cope, the more rationally you will be able to deal with difficult emotions, and the stronger these positive pathways will become in your brain.

Learning how to shift from outside to inside your window can be a powerful tool to building not just your ability to self-regulate, but also in becoming more comfortable in your body and feeling confident in your ability to navigate the emotional terrain of your relationships.

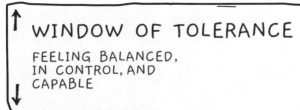

HYPERAROUSAL

FEELING ANGRY,
ANXIOUS, + A DESIRE
TO RUN AWAY

DYSREGULATION

WINDOW OF TOLERANCE

FEELING BALANCED,
IN CONTROL, AND
CAPABLE

DYSREGULATION

HYPOAROUSAL

FEELING FLAT,
NUMB, FATIGUED,
+ DEPRESSED

MENTAL NOTES

Take five minutes at the end of each day for a month to reflect on the following:

* Upon reflection, where am I in relation to my window of tolerance today? (E.g. I feel content so I'm within my window. I feel really anxious so I think I'm above it.)

* What circumstances may have contributed toward this, both positive and negative? (E.g. A great sleep, a dull day, conflict with a loved one.)

* What story did I attach to the above circumstances? Is it possible this narrative has also contributed to my current emotional state? (E.g. The story I am telling myself about what happened is my partner doesn't love me anymore, I'm being taken for granted ...)

* Going forward, what can I remind myself of that would help me in these circumstances? (E.g. I can remind myself that the story is not fact. I can remind myself that today is one day and tomorrow will be different.)

After the month, you'll have heaps of information at your fingertips about how you react to things and why, including ideas of how you can improve this moving forward.

5.
Self-
Regulation

HOW TO SOOTHE
YOURSELF

"It's not about feeling better, it's about getting better at feeling."
Gabor Maté

Would you describe yourself as a perfectionist? In times of anger, do you react in the heat of the moment rather than with a conscious, considered response? Perhaps you withdraw entirely? Do you turn to food, alcohol, or substances in moments of high stress? Do you often experience high levels of shame? If so, it's likely that the information in this chapter will be helpful for you. Self-regulation is a skill—and not one I've come by naturally. If, like me, you've frequently struggled with anxiety or issues like the ones I just mentioned, it's likely that your regulation skills could do with a bit of conscious care and attention.

SO WHAT IS SELF-REGULATION?

Self-regulation, specifically emotional self-regulation, is our ability to willfully reduce the intensity of our emotions and bring ourselves back within the "window of tolerance" that we talked about in the previous chapter.

Typically, we learn how to do this through our parents, or caregivers, in an interactive process called co-regulation. This occurs when an adult provides an emotionally safe environment for a child, is warm and responsive to them, and demonstrates self-regulation in their *own* behaviors.

In infancy, children require adults to fulfill a large portion of their regulatory needs such as feeding, cleanliness, and management of their environmental stimuli. We also rely, as infants, on our caregivers to be sensitive to our emotional cues and to soothe us in times of distress. We then maintain certain aspects of this need for co-regulation as we get older, particularly during the chaotic period we call the teens. Effective co-regulation therefore sets a person up to healthily deal with the range of intense emotions they are likely to experience throughout their lifetime. Unfortunately, however, not everyone receives optimal co-regulation in childhood. And, unlike children, who are seen as "still learning," adults are more often than not simply expected to just know how to do things.

As such, even if we haven't had a healthy model of self-regulation early on in our lives, we're usually expected to just know how to manage our anxiety, our anger, and all our other emotions—in a way that is not only socially palatable, but that is also beneficial to our well-being and our relationships.

HOW AND WHEN TO SELF-REGULATE

The good news is that we are never too old to grow our capacity to handle difficult emotions. In the absence of early modeling, there are many practical exercises that can be done to encourage self-regulation.

Thinking back to the window of tolerance explained in the previous chapter, we saw that when we stray outside this window, we tend to fall into a state of either hyperarousal and/or hypo-arousal. Each of these states needs a different type of approach to help regulate it:

* With hyperarousal, we need ways to down-regulate—ways to slow down.
* With hypo-arousal, we need ways to up-regulate—ways to bring a healthy dose of anxiety (yes, there is such a thing!) or excitement.

As you read through the practices, you'll notice an arrow beside each. Those with an arrow pointing down will be helpful for heightened moments when in need of down-regulation. Those with an arrow pointing up are for when we're feeling slumped and need some up-regulating. Those with both an up and a down arrow can be effective in both contexts. The onus is on us to recognize what it is we need and then to implement the most relevant practices in our everyday lives.

Those of us with a well-established sense of self are also likely to notice internal signals such as spiraling thoughts, the thinking traps talked about in Chapter 3, shallow breathing, stomach cramps, and all sorts of other "symptoms." As with any symptoms, once we notice them, we can take the steps that we know from experience will help to stop these feelings from escalating.

However, if co-regulation was never modeled for us as children, we might have developed ways to try to regulate, as adults, that add to our emotional load rather than alleviate it, such as always keeping busy, overcommitting and overworking, procrastinating, or even turning to substances to take the edge off things or to numb out. In the short term, it may not feel like some of these well-worn techniques are harmful but, as time passes, we can find ourselves in a more anxious and distraught position than we were in to begin with. Developing the skill of healthy regulation is therefore a key contributor to mental well-being.

The body instinctively knows the importance of self-regulation. Here are just some ways the body intuitively discharges and recovers from stress and strain:

* Crying
* Laughing
* Giggling
* Shaking
* Sighing
* Stomach gurgling
* Waves of heat and/or chills
* Sweating
* Tingling
* Yawning
* Deeper breathing

In order to regulate our emotional well-being, we first need to have an awareness of our own emotional state, and our response to stimuli. This is the foundation of self-regulation. When we know ourselves better, we have the ability to reflect and choose a route that feels right for us. Annoyingly, we often find that the right path is rarely the most comfortable.

When we're what is called "dysregulated," we're at a greater risk of sacrificing our boundaries and saying yes when we mean no. We're more inclined to feel the pull of old patterns and coping mechanisms.

When, on the other hand, we're regulated, we can meet the pull of old patterns and the like with a stronger energy, staying with what we think, or what we know, is true and authentic for us.

But staying rooted in our authenticity isn't always easy. Oftentimes, it requires a lot of attention, especially at the beginning of our journey, or when there might be an opposing energy from someone we love.

In addition, when we're triggered or doing the hard work of unpacking difficult parts of our life experiences, we edge closer and closer to the edge of our window of tolerance—and sometimes right out the window! Hence the need for emotional and physical soothing becomes even stronger.

In order to tend to the unhealed parts of ourselves, we must be at a place of safety within ourselves. This doesn't necessarily mean a place of comfort; rather, safety means knowing that we can soothe ourselves when we need to—that we can rely on ourselves to take care of many of our own needs, both physical and emotional.

WHEN WE'RE DYSREGULATED, WE'RE AT A GREATER RISK OF SACRIFICING OUR BOUNDARIES AND SAYING YES WHEN WE MEAN NO.

INTRODUCING SELF-REGULATION PRACTICES

In the pages that follow, you will find a generous offering of self-regulation practices—both a wide range of grounding practices (including both breath work and sensory techniques, among other things) and of creative rituals. Some are suitable for down-regulation and others for up-regulation. If you think about it practically, down-regulation practices will calm, focus, and ground. Up-regulation will usually bring about a form of movement and creativity.

Be aware that, as I mentioned toward the end of the last chapter, bringing attention to the inner experience of the body without the guidance of a trained mental health professional—whether through breath or sensory work, for example—can at times do more harm than good for some people with histories of trauma. So, if you're concerned about this, you may want to consider seeking a professional to support you in this kind of work.

However, as you read on, you'll see that there are many exercise options to help bring a sense of calm such as basic mindfulness guidance, where you simply observe your surroundings and also a range of creative endeavors.

Note to self: Self-regulation doesn't have to mean sitting still in silence! Nor does it have to be carried out alone. Being around others who are safe and regulated can help us to regulate our own distress, too. So please do reach out if and when you need to.

And, as ever, allow your practice to grow, move, deepen, and change as you do.

GROUNDING PRACTICES

The range of grounding practices in the pages that follow are helpful any time in day-to-day life but they become particularly invaluable when you're feeling anxious, stressed, overwhelmed, floaty, disconnected, angry, panicked, or caught up in distressing thoughts, behaviors, feelings, or memories.

They can also help to bring you away from the "there and then" of your past experiences, and into the safety of the here and now, which means that they can be particularly helpful in situations in which you catch yourself engaged in thinking traps, experiencing flashbacks, or waking up from a distressing dream.

The grounding exercises that follow require you to keep your eyes open unless otherwise specified—and to regularly check in with your senses. The body is the greatest doorway to connection with the present moment.

The practices can be done anywhere that you feel safe and comfortable, although some people feel that they gain more benefit from them when they are able to find a quiet space where they can sit undisturbed while doing them.

Take as much time as you have, or want to take, for each practice that you choose to do. But even if you only have a few minutes for any one exercise, you will start to experience differences in how you feel if you continue this regularly.

Practices that work for someone else might not work for you. So just read through the different practices on offer and circle any and all that catch your attention, or that you feel might work for you. And then try them out to see how you go.

As mentioned in the previous chapter, it is useful to try the practices even when you're *not* actively experiencing distress, as if you get used to a practice before you need it, it will be more accessible to you in difficult moments.

Engage with your practice of choice as thoroughly as you can on any given day. This will vary, and that's OK. Allow it to. Close each practice by bringing your awareness back to the safety of the present, to the room you're in, the sounds, the colors, the surroundings, taking a moment to prepare for the rest of your day.

5-4-3-2-1 Senses Technique

By doing this grounding 5-4-3-2-1 senses technique, you will consciously take in details of your environment using your senses that you might usually skim over or tune out, allowing you to connect to your environment in a healthier, more mindful way than you normally do.

1. Take a long deep breath.
2. Note and name five things you can see around you.
3. Note and name four things you can touch around you.
4. Note and name three things you can hear outside your body.
5. Note and name two things you can smell.
6. Note and name one thing you can taste.

4-4-4 Breath Technique

The 4-4-4 breath technique is a quick and accessible method to bring a felt sense of calm to your mind and body in times of worry and anxiety.

1. Start by placing your feet on the floor and straightening your back.
2. Inhale for a slow count of 1, 2, 3, 4.
3. Hold your breath for the count of 1, 2, 3, 4.
4. Exhale for the count of 1, 2, 3, 4.
5. Repeat for 2 minutes.

Sensory Techniques

Focusing on the physicality of our senses has the power to bring us into the present moment, particularly when we turn our full attention to them, one by one. For example, how often in everyday life do we look at one thing while holding or touching another thing, or listen to a podcast while simultaneously eating something, for example? Most of us use our senses as a backing track to our lives, whereas the practices below allow us to view them as the main events.

Sight Practices
Below are three engaging sight-based practices that can help to bring you more into the here and now when required. Choose whichever one you feel most drawn to and aim to practice it once a day.

* Allow your eyes and focus to soften. Inhale and follow the journey of the breath. Notice as it enters your nose and reaches all the way down into the lungs. As you exhale, trace the breath leaving your body. Notice when it releases from the lungs, the nose, and the mouth. Spend five minutes observing the breath in this way, really acknowledging this incredible mechanism of your body.
* Look around at the objects in your immediate environment such as ornaments, pictures, fabrics, and items of furniture. Pick one to focus on, really observe it, and describe it in your own head in detail. Note the colors, textures, shapes, patterns etc. And see if it changes how you feel about the object you are looking at and the space you are in.
* Sitting or standing, simply look at your feet. Start with your attention at the bottom of your ankles, move it slowly to the bottom of your feet, then to the tops, and finally to the toes. Pay close attention to each area in turn, and note any sensations.

Sound Practices

Below are a couple of sounding anchors that can bring us into the here and now. Choose whichever one you feel most drawn to and aim to practice it once a day.

* Put on a song of your choosing. Either sitting or standing, simply listen to and concentrate on the music as it unfurls around you. Any time you feel an urge to do something else at the same time, whether look out the window or check your phone, gently bring your attention back to the sound. What do you notice in your body as you listen? Take this one song's worth of time to simply "be."

* Try ASMR, which stands for Autonomous Sensory Meridian Response. Don't worry if you've never heard of this. You're not alone. One way of describing it is as the tingling sensation (or "brain massage") that you sometimes get in the scalp, neck, back, and arms in response to both audio and visual triggers, such as whispering, scratching, and tapping.

Research has found that roughly 20 percent of the world's population experience strong ASMR. So look into it online and see what you think; and if one style of ASMR doesn't work for you, feel free to experiment with others. Although in the infancy stage of scientific research, feedback so far is indicating that it can help significantly with relaxation, stress relief, and insomnia.

Scent Practices

Below are two appealing scent-based practices that can help to bring you deeper into the present moment when you feel the need. Choose whichever one you feel most drawn to and aim to practice it once a day:

* Source a scented candle that you love. Whether you're drawn to earthy scents like moss and turf or you enjoy clean laundry or sugar cookie, pick one that you enjoy. Find a quiet space to sit and light the candle. Watch as the wax begins to melt. Note as the smell begins to reach you. Is it constant? Does it waver? How would you describe it?
* Pick up a book that's dear to your heart and bring the pages up to your nose. Breathe in, and as you do, notice the scent of the pages. What does it smell like?

What do you notice in your body as you do this? The process works wonderfully with either old or new books—just whatever you have at your disposal.

Taste Practice

Below is an in-depth taste-based practice that can help to bring you deeper into the present moment when desired. Alone time + chocolate = grounding I can get on board with. So:

1. Source some chocolate and find a quiet, comfortable place (away from quick-handed, chocolate-loving relatives!).
2. Take a small piece of chocolate in your hand.
3. Spend a few moments just breathing and being aware of how it feels to be here, now.
4. Bring your attention to the chocolate in your hand. Note the shape, the color, and any responses you have to it.
5. Bring it to your nose and notice what scent first connects with you. Is it stronger than expected? Is it subtle?
6. Notice any urges you feel to gobble it down and gently bring your focus back to the piece in your hand. Know that the rest of the chocolate is there for you afterward if you wish, but right now, you're going to focus on just this piece for the purposes of grounding.
7. Now place the piece of chocolate in your mouth and notice what tastes and flavors emerge. Hold it in your mouth for as long as possible, noticing as it melts, and exploring the unfolding texture and tastes.

8. When it is gone, bring your attention back to your sense of taste. How strong is the taste now?

9. Bring your attention back to your breath and body. Rest here, being aware of how you feel. Is it different to how you felt at the start of the practice?

Touch Practices

Below are several touch-based practices that can help to bring you more fully into the present moment when you feel you need it. Choose whichever one you feel most drawn to and aim to practice it once a day:

* Touch an item near you. Can you pick it up? If so, note its weight. Is it heavy or light? What about its temperature? Does it feel warm or cold? Or does it vary? Note the texture. How specific can you be? Once you've observed and explored the item in full, put it back where you found it, noticing any emotions or sensations that you have had during the process.

* Get an ice cube from the freezer and hold it in your hand. How does it feel in the beginning? Cold, and what else? How long before it starts to melt? Does the sensation of holding it change as it begins to melt? Does it feel the same in each part of your hand? Focus on the temperature and how it feels on your fingertips, then on the back of your hands, then on your palms. Holding ice in our hands is a speedy and effective way to bring our awareness back into the present moment as the coldness of the ice demands our focused attention.

* Try putting your hands in a basin of cold water and taking note of the sensations you experience. If you feel comfortable to do so, then alternate

your hands between this cold water and some warm water, taking note of the differences in sensation that the two experiences cause.

A Tapping Practice

Sometimes, when we're in a state of hypo-arousal (see page 145 in Chapter 4), we need a grounding technique that "awakens" us somewhat—bringing heightened awareness and life into the body. A technique called "tapping" (also known as EFT, or Emotional Freedom Technique) is a simple, effective method that can be used at any time.

Below is a tapping routine specifically designed to bring the heightened awareness that we just talked of above into your whole body:

1. Start by tapping the back of your left hand with the palm and fingers of your right hand, using firm but gentle gestures, at a rate of roughly two taps a second. There's no need to be too exact with this as it's merely an attempt to convey the pace of taps you should be aiming for.
2. When you've got a sense of the rhythm, start the process of spending about 30 seconds tapping on each main area of the body, one by one. After the first 30 seconds tapping the left hand, move up to the forearm, tapping first the top of it, then underneath. Then move up the upper arm and do the same.
3. Next, move to the left shoulder, the left side of the chest, and, as you make your way down the left side of the body, use your left hand to tap the back of your body in unison with *right* hand tapping the front.

4. Work down the rest of the left side of the body: the waist, the hip, the bum, the thigh, the calf, the foot.
5. Then, after you've finished the left-hand side, stand tall and notice what you can feel. Does the left side of the body feel any different to the right? If so, in what way? What sensations are present on the left, and on the right? What words would you use to describe each side?
6. Take a moment to feel into the sensations of the body, and when you're ready, begin the whole process again on the right side, with the left hand.
7. After you've tapped the right side of the body, stand tall again and take notice of how the body feels.

Take 5: Consider What Calm Is to You

Ask yourself the following questions:

* What does "calm" look like to me?

* What does calm feel like to me?

* What colors, images, tastes, and sensations come to mind when I think of being calm?

Take some time to write these in your journal, in your phone, or wherever is handiest for you.

MINDFULNESS PRACTICE

It's no coincidence that all the grounding practices presented so far incorporate the practice of mindfulness. One of the core purposes of mindfulness is to heighten your awareness of life as it unfolds around you.

Some people might experience resistance to the word mindfulness, and that's OK. It's understandable given the level of attention the practice has been given in recent years and the subsequent overuse of the term.

If you're approaching mindfulness with an air of skepticism, there's no need to worry! I found myself in a similar position during my psychotherapy training and, when I confessed this to my skills lecturer, she replied "Great! I love when this happens. You'll find the most benefit from it, in time." I nodded politely, not fully trusting her. But unsurprisingly (I can say in hindsight), she was entirely correct. What at first I had believed to be a bit "fluffy," a bit "woo-woo" or "alternative," is now an invaluable practice that I draw on daily.

Mindfulness is not:

* Having no thoughts or attempting to achieve a blank state of mind
* An attempt to get rid of unwanted experiences
* About never being distracted
* Focusing on the positives and ignoring discomfort
* Something only achievable through meditation and changing your lifestyle

Mindfulness *is*:

* Becoming aware of what emotions, sensations, and thoughts are present
* Experiencing the present moment as it is
* Gently and consciously realigning the mind **when** (not if!) it becomes distracted
* A way to grow our capacity to "be" with uncomfortable emotions
* A step toward accepting things as they are, not as how we wish them to be

For example, as I write this, I'm outside. It's a sunny Wednesday morning. There's a blue sky, a light breeze, and a flock of birds swirling in formation around a tower on a quiet day in the heart of Dublin city. I can already feel that this moment has replenished me from my yesterday and nourished me for my day ahead. And that's all mindfulness is. Engaging in the present moment. Taking stock of the senses, the body, and the breath as they are, as they're experiencing, in this moment.

There is no right or wrong way to practice. The aim isn't to sit through a mindfulness exercise without distraction. It is to notice and gently bring yourself back to the present moment when the mind wanders. (Note that I say "when" the mind wanders, not "if" the mind wanders, as the wandering is inevitable for us all!)

Take 5: Be Mindful with This Book

Can you use this book as the object of a mindfulness practice now that you know what is meant by the concept of mindfulness? Just place the book in your lap, continue to read it, and take time to experience your present moment, breath by breath, if it feels safe to do so. How does this make you feel?

Let the Sound Unfold

1. Find a comfortable spot and gently close your eyes. If it feels more comfortable for you, simply turn your gaze downward, and keep a soft focus.
2. Tune in to the sounds around you. Let them enter your awareness. If you're sitting inside, notice the noises within the room. Perhaps the sound of a clock, the creak of a door, footsteps in another room. And also notice the noises outside. Perhaps the sound of traffic, birds, people talking, the breeze, or the rain against the window. Without holding on to any of the sounds, simply notice each one and allow it to slip by. The only thing you need to be in this moment is an observer of sound.
3. You may notice that the mind begins to wander, or it may attach to certain sounds, becoming invested in the story of the sound. When you notice this, gently return, without judgment—simply noticing and letting go. Take as much time here as you would like.

An Invitation To My Selves

Nowadays, we're lucky if we're ever able to give our full attention to one task, as there are always so many different tasks to be done and so many different hats to wear. A practice I like to do with my clients is called "An Invitation To My Selves":

1. Find a quiet place to sit, or put your headphones on and turn on some meditation music, a favorite relaxing tune or some lo-fi beats on YouTube. When you're comfortable, close your eyes or turn your gaze downward, keeping a soft focus.

2. Take note of the breath, as it is. Where is it reaching?

3. Allow a deep breath of air in and feel your tummy expand, and your chest rise.

4. After sitting watching the breath traveling in and out, in and out, for a minute, notice where your mind is wandering to.

5. Now gently invite all the different parts of yourself to put down their multitasking hats, and come into the present moment. There may be parts of our mind that are caught up in work, parts that are thinking about the commute, parts that have gone ahead and are thinking about something you have to do later, what's on the menu for dinner this evening, what to do with the kids this weekend, or what's on the TV tonight.

6. Recognize each part and gently invite them all to come in to the here and now, knowing that they can return to these separate places soon. Are there parts that come willingly? Are there parts that are reluctant to set down their hat for a moment? Avoid any judging or criticizing; simply invite and notice.

7. Take some moments here and when you feel ready, gently open your eyes.

A Teatime Ritual

"I don't have the time" and "I'm too busy" are phrases that have often left my mouth.
I constantly used to feel that I didn't have the space in my day to slow down and take
a moment for myself because of X, Y, and oh yes, dreaded Z (even though I'd still
manage to somehow find a way to scroll for a few hours on my phone in the evening
and dive headfirst into the latest British procedural or box set).

By failing to make this time for myself, what I was really doing was placing myself
in a situation that left me open to increased dysregulation, increased stress, and an
increased likelihood to snap at those around me for the most trivial of things.

A beloved but blunt mate of mine said one evening as I bemoaned how difficult
I was finding a module I was taking: "How can you not have time when you make
yourself four cups of tea a morning?"

She was teasing, but I heard her message loud and clear. I *did* have time; I just
wasn't designating it appropriately.

I was drifting away, caught up in the story of what I "should" do instead of
concentrating on what I needed.

A simple way I then began to intentionally introduce more presence, slowness, and
calm into my life was creating a ritual out of my tea-making.

Making a cup of tea is one of those activities that we usually do on autopilot.
Think about it. Can you recall the last time you boiled the kettle? What else can you
remember from that moment? If you're anything like me, chances are your mind was
on the busy morning ahead or behind you, what's left on the list of things to do, that
embarrassing thing you said ten years ago, or what you'll snack on alongside it.

But mindful tea-making and drinking is a humble meditative practice that is available to us all—a humdrum daily activity the nature of which can change completely if undertaken mindfully. And don't worry if tea isn't your beverage of choice; coffee, herbal tea, hot chocolate, or any other such drink will do the job just as well.

Here's how to create a grounding ritual out of this simple act:

1. Put the kettle on and simply be present. As you notice other thoughts or distractions crop up, gently come back to what is happening in the present moment. You have nothing else to do right now. You have nowhere else to be.
2. Place your tea bag into your favorite mug.
3. Once the kettle boils, pour the water over the tea bag. Listen to the sound of the water as it lands on the tea, as it fills the cup.
4. Observe as the tea bag begins to expand and fill out.
5. Notice the color of the water—is there any change? Can you name the color?
6. Note the shapes that rise from the steam in the mug.
7. Find a quiet, comfortable place to sit with your tea.
8. Take a deep breath in through your nose and exhale through your mouth. Imagine the breath reaching right down into your toes and, as you exhale, visualize all stress and tension leaving your body.
9. Feel the cup beneath your fingertips. What do you notice? Is it smooth, or rough?
10. Hold your cup under your nose. What can you smell? You don't need to be an aficionado or a tea-sommelier. It's OK if you can't detect the supposed subtle hints of jasmine and tobacco. Just notice what's there. Does it smell sweet? Earthy? Floral?

11. Take in the feel of the cup on your lips and the feeling of the tea as you take your first mouthful. With each sip, feel the warmth as the tea moves from your mouth to your throat to your stomach.
12. Rest here, taking in and savoring each mouthful and the experience of your senses in the moment.

Wrap Up

This simple but effective way of comforting yourself is a big hit with many of my clients. You'll see why in a moment! If you'd like to, you can set a gentle alarm on your phone for fifteen minutes, but just work with whatever time you have.

1. Lie or sit somewhere quiet and comfortable, and wrap yourself in a duvet or a blanket.
2. As you rest with the cover wrapped around you, bring your attention to what you are doing, and the snug and cozy feeling of the cocoon around you.
3. As the mind wanders or thoughts pop up, don't fight them. Just gently guide your awareness back to the present moment, the feel of the duvet or blanket, and the sensation of being protected in a safe haven.

Giving Gratitude

Many studies now show that when we adopt an attitude of gratitude and incorporate it into our daily life, it can decrease stress, improve health, and orient us toward the positives in our lives, which can otherwise be easily overlooked in the hustle and bustle of our days.

1. Find a quiet, comfortable spot, where you can sit, reflect, and write in your journal or a notebook.

2. Take some time to note all the things you feel grateful for today. These might include the weather, having a day off, your health, certain friendships …The things on your list can be as general or specific as you wish.

3. Try and include at least one thing that felt personal to you today. This might be the joy as that first sip of coffee touched your soul this morning, or the breeze through your fingers as you walked home this evening. Take time to consider the details of these experiences, and jot them down.

4. Now read through what you have written and internally thank each of these experiences for being a part of your life today. Feel free to place your hands on your heart if it helps.

5. Once you're done, bring your focus into the present moment. How does it feel to be here, practicing gratitude? What do you notice in your body? Breathe deeply and be, just for a moment, with nothing to do but sit with gratitude.

CREATIVE RITUALS

Putting a pen, pencil, or paintbrush to paper can be another great way to not only self-soothe and self-regulate but also to let any thoughts or emotions out.

And there's no need to worry if you're no Picasso or Shakespeare! Creative practices can prove a wonderful release, regardless of our artistic capabilities! There are no rules to the flow of the ink or the swish of the brush. So don't overthink it. In fact, the less thinking the better. Simply allow yourself to engage in the creative practices below and know that any messages within will be there when you're ready to see them.

Back to the Future

Get out a pen and paper and write a letter to the person you are right now, from the future you in two years' time. Write about your life as it looks in two years, being as detailed as possible! Include information on the people you have around you, the things you have done, the hopes you had that have become a reality, and what life looks like living as the true you. What does your day look like? What does it feel like? What compassionate guidance might the future you offer your present-day self?

Inspiration from the Sky

Sometimes, to replenish our energy and rebalance ourselves, we need a healthy dose of escapism and fantasy. Daydreaming and storytelling are far from being worthless distractions; they're an essential human activity that can make us feel vibrant, engaged, and grounded.

Rather than zoning out with something on the TV, take some paper and a pen, or your laptop, and see where your stream of thought takes you with one of the sky-based creative writing prompts below. Try not to overthink it. Just allow yourself to be surprised.

THIS IS
YOUR GENTLE
REMINDER TO
NAME ONE THING,
IN THIS MOMENT,
YOU FEEL GRATEFUL
FOR

* *The night sky was alive…*
* *The remains of the summer sun faded from sight…*
* *The sun rose in its predictable way, giving no indication that today was the day I had wished for…*

↑ Craft a Touchstone

It can be powerful to keep something close to us that represents a sense of calm and that can act as a reminder to take a breath when we're feeling overwhelmed or anxious. And even nicer if you can create something that is personal to you, so let's create our very own "touchstone."

1. Take a deep breath in, hold it, and exhale. What is that sensation like—of the deep exhale? What symbol, image, or color comes to mind when you exhale deeply? Perhaps it's the sea, a book, the sun, a chair…?
2. With whatever resources you have at your disposal (be it paint, coloring pencils, charcoals, crayons…), draw a picture of this symbol or image—as simple or as detailed as you wish. Take as much time on this as you want.
3. Once you've completed your image, place it somewhere close by where you'll come into contact with it several times a day.
4. Then each time you see it, this image will stand as an invitation to calm and re-ground yourself—a touchstone for stressful moments when they appear. A soft reminder to inhale for 4, hold for 4, and exhale for 4.

Drops of Sunshine

1. Source an empty jar, preferably one you like the look of.
2. Then, whenever something good, nourishing, or uplifting happens, take a scrap of paper and jot down what it was. There's no need to go into too much detail—just enough to trigger the memory.
3. As you write your experience down, visualize the color and the joy of each of these moments. Notice how the joy seeps into the scraps of paper, not taking from your felt sense of joy, but growing it and making it more plentiful. Your written notes can be as simple or as detailed, as straightforward or as elaborate as you wish—anything from going on a holiday to the first crunch of the autumn leaves under your feet.
4. Place these notes, or, as I like to call them, your "drops of sunshine," into the jar.
5. Then, any time you're having a tough day, pick one, two, or more "drops of sunshine" out and read through them, allowing the positive feelings that emerge from the memories to replenish you once more.

Darragh's Dog

In a recent post on my Instagram page @TheMindGeek, I asked my followers how they show themselves safety when faced with anxiety. An old friend of mine called Darragh left a comment that resonated with many people:

Something I've started to do recently is to treat my anxiety like a dog barking out of a window, in that I know it's making a mountain out of a molehill, but I make sure it feels heard and that it knows it's done its job.

Following Darragh's example above, if you imagined your anxiety as a dog, what would your harried hound look like? What breed would it be? What name might it have? What could you say to your dog when it begins to yap and bark?

Next time you're feeling particularly anxious, consider how you could make your perturbed pet feel heard and affirmed for the work he is doing looking out for you—and if needed, consider taking him outside for some fresh air.

↑ Art Attack: Home Edition

For this exercise, you'll need a piece of paper (preferably 11×17 or ledger size), a paper plate, and your paints. Feel free to improvise!

1. Grab your paper plate and squeeze your paint out onto it, choosing as many colors as you're drawn to, being sure to place each color apart from each other.
2. When you've placed your chosen colors on the plate, begin to rotate the plate on its side and watch as the colors weave, blend, and merge together. Observe the intricate interlacing of the colors—the beautiful patterns they make.
3. When you're ready, bring your plate over to your piece of paper, turn the plate on its side, and allow the paint to spill and drip onto the paper.

4. Move the plate about if you wish, allowing your hand to guide the paint as it falls.
5. Observe your design on the paper. Do you want to add anything extra? Do you want to go in with your fingertips or leave it as it is? Do what feels intuitive for you, allowing this moment to be about nothing more than you and the paint.
6. When you're finished, take some deep breaths as you look at your painting. How do you feel now? How did you feel before? Allow whatever comes.

Take 5: Identify Your Hurdles

Learning to self-soothe and self-regulate isn't easy. Our mind and body often want the path of least resistance—what is comfortable and familiar. So it's completely normal if when we begin to incorporate new practices it feels like an uphill struggle at first.

Resistance isn't only normal; it's a sign that you're pushing against and breaking an old pattern. But the object isn't to push ourselves into overwhelm or to avoid difficult emotions altogether; rather it is to sit with and experience the mild discomfort of growth. So keep this in mind and carry on …

LEARNING HOW TO SELF-REGULATE CAN BE DIFFICULT IF:

IT WASN'T MODELED FOR YOU AS A CHILD

YOU'RE OVERWORKED, SICK, OR BURNED OUT

YOU CONSISTENTLY THINK OTHER PEOPLE SHOULD CHANGE

YOU DON'T CREATE TIME TO REFLECT

YOU'RE RELUCTANT TO LEARN NEW WAYS OF COPING

MENTAL NOTES

Take five minutes at the end of each day for a month to reflect on the following:

* What hurdles might be getting in the way for me? How might I be able to overcome these hurdles?
* How can I offer my thoughts and my body some understanding? What is it I want them to know?
* Why is it important that I learn how to regulate? Can I communicate this in the kind way I would to a child?

After the month, you'll have pages of insight into what hurdles stand in the way of your regulation practice, what needs you have on a daily basis, what it is you want from your new coping skills, as well as a reminder as to why regulation is important for you.

6.
Setting
Boundaries

HOW TO PRACTICE GENUINE SELF-CARE

"Responsibility to yourself means refusing to let others
do your thinking, talking, and naming for you . . ."
Adrienne Rich

The term "self-care" is thrown around a lot these days—so much so that its meaning has become somewhat hazy and skewed. As such, it would be entirely understandable if you rolled your eyes or felt a bit "meh" about the concept. Due to overuse and commercialization of the term, it can be difficult to discern between genuine self-care and "hashtag self-care." Yet we shouldn't write it off, as genuine self-care has an important role to play in our lives, and in our wellness.

CONNECTING BOUNDARIES AND SELF-CARE

Setting boundaries doesn't typically spring to mind when most of us think about self-care and yet it's one of the most effective ways we can truly care for ourselves and others. When we understand that boundaries create, maintain, and honor our own limits as well as others,' we will be able to take care of ourselves in a way that no amount of bubble baths could ever do.

In essence, boundaries mark our limits, whether they be emotional, psychological, energetic, or physical. They keep us protected, they help us to feel safe in relationships, and they teach those in our world how we would like them to interact with us. Holding or sticking to our boundaries enables us to protect ourselves from burnout, harmful behavior, and resentment. And also allows us to maintain our sense of agency and to separate who we are from the identity, thoughts, and behaviors of others.

When implemented in a healthy way, boundaries require us to take responsibility for our own actions and emotions, while ensuring that we do not carry the emotional weight, or undertake the emotional labor, of others.

The Benefits of Boundaries

* They keep us safe
* They enable us to take responsibility for what is ours and ours only
* They allow others the opportunity to take responsibility for themselves

* They improve the health of our relationships
* They improve our relationship with intimacy
* They help us avoid feeling manipulated, resentful, or taken for granted
* They help us determine who we wish to let into our lives and to what extent
* They help us maintain a clear distinction between our own feelings, thoughts, identity, and those of others
* They model for little ones (and indeed adult ones) how they deserve to be treated

UNDERSTANDING BOUNDARIES

We learn about boundaries by what is modeled for us in childhood, as well as from our peer groups throughout our lives. If our parents didn't set healthy boundaries, we may also have difficulty setting them for ourselves. Likewise, some families or cultures place a high value on individualism and personal space whereas others will place a high value on community and are more collectivist in nature.

We tend to unconsciously repeat the boundary patterns we learned at an early age. That is, until we encounter a situation or person who has different ideas about what a boundary is. For example, if we spend a lot of our energy spreading ourselves thin and trying to meet the needs of others just like our main caregiver has done during our childhood, it can come as quite a shock when we hear someone else in a similar situation say, "I won't be able to do that. It's been a busy week, so I'm taking the weekend to rest." Our initial reaction might be one of utter horror. *Can they do that?*

Because they're tired?! I haven't been anything but tired since 2006 and I still say yes/don't cancel!

As a result, someone honoring their *own* needs by stating specific boundaries or wishes can feel jarring at times and bring up a lot of emotion. This can highlight that our own boundaries could do with some care and attention.

Securing Your Front Door

As a visual learner, I love any metaphor that will help better my understanding of a concept. In order to clarify our definition of boundaries, it can be useful to picture them as the front door to your house.

When we leave our front door wide open (i.e. have no boundaries), anything or anyone is liable to come in, stay for however long they wish, and take whatever they want, as it has been left to them to make assumptions about what we're OK with.

However, when we close the door (i.e. have a firm boundary in place), people have to knock at the door or ring the bell to let us know they're there, and we can then choose who or what to let in and who or what to leave outside. This way we have the chance to say "I'm not free right now" or "Yes, come in," according to our current circumstance, rather than getting ourselves into situations we don't want to be in.

Take 5: Assess Your Boundaries

To get a better measure of where you are with you own boundary-setting in life, ask yourself the following questions:

* Do I have trouble saying no?
* Do I feel guilt or shame when I can't do something for someone else?
* Do I over-share?
* Do I think of boundaries as selfish or indulgent?
* Do I try to fix things for others?
* Do I take on the responsibilities of others?
* Do I have trouble making decisions?
* Do I do favors that I later feel resentment over?
* Am I a "rescuer"?
* Do I frequently blame others for how I'm feeling or for how I reacted?
* Do I often feel taken advantage of?
* Do I find it difficult to know where my thoughts/feelings end and another's begin?
* Do I frequently worry about disappointing others?
* Do I find myself exhausted after spending time with certain people?

If you answered "Yes" to many or all of the above, it is likely that your boundaries could do with some maintenance and loving care.

TYPES OF BOUNDARIES

There are three types of personal boundary:

* Rigid
* Porous
* Healthy

Rigid Boundaries

Rigid boundaries function akin to walls by keeping others firmly away and keeping us firmly in. If our boundaries are rigid, we may have a hard time asking for help and we may struggle with intimacy and close relationships.

If you recognize this in yourself, you may want to reflect on any fears that crop up at the thought of letting someone in or seeing who you really are.

Porous Boundaries

With porous boundaries, the front door is wide open or even taken off the hinges entirely when it comes to letting people in. We may over-share personal information, struggle to say no, and/or feel responsible for the emotions of others. We often accept disrespectful behavior, whether we mean to or not, and are fearful of not being liked.

If you can see yourself in this description, it is likely you could benefit from strengthening your boundaries with others. You may want to start by reflecting on what factors might be holding you back from setting your own healthy limits.

Healthy Boundaries

People with healthy boundaries are somewhere in the middle of the above two extremes in that they are able to say "no" without guilt. They communicate their wants and needs, and they choose to let in only those they wish. They don't compromise their values and they accept the decisions of others.

As with most things, the key is balance. As such, we need to ensure that we're neither a prisoner of rigidity nor a sufferer of porous boundaries. That said, in the early stage of setting boundaries, it's better to be on the rigid end than the porous. Rigid boundaries are not necessarily unhealthy; in fact, there are situations in which they can be very useful. For example, if we had a domineering parent who always told us what to do or ridiculed or gaslighted us, it makes sense that we would be very selective and have rigid boundaries about who we're open to sharing our perspective with.

Some boundaries can be more obvious than others such as how much time we spend with someone or how much we choose to share with someone. Other boundaries may not be so clear until we've gone beyond them. These more subtle boundaries could include, for example, the amount of news and social media we consume, the length of time we're willing to listen to other people venting or sharing their pain, when a family member gossips about another family member, or a friend continues to show up unannounced.

The key to understanding where boundaries are required comes from you, first and foremost.

COMMON BOUNDARY MISCONCEPTIONS

If you've ever worried about saying no, or felt it wasn't an option, you're not alone. The desire to "keep the peace" whatever the cost is often perpetuated by messages we internalize somewhere along the line growing up. If you're concerned that setting boundaries will harm your relationships, don't worry. Let's take a look at some of the myths that we tend to buy into which keep us from communicating our limits.

Misconception 1: Boundaries Push People Away

The most common misconception about boundaries is the idea that they push people away. Ironically, instead of doing this, boundaries are mostly implemented in order to do the very opposite: create connection and intimacy in the long run, be that within friendships, within romantic relationships, within families, or elsewhere. This is because boundaries are all about showing both trust and respect for ourselves and others.

As such, setting healthy limits on how much we allow people or situations through our front door and for what length of time is simply about respecting our own needs, preservation of our own mental health, and acknowledgment of the sometimes difficult fact that not every relationship in our life will *always* be conducive to our well-being.

Misconception 2: Boundaries Are Selfish

Setting boundaries can feel selfish when we care deeply about others and want to maintain the peace in our relationships, but every relationship needs boundaries to be healthy and balanced. The only people who are likely to make us feel that setting boundaries is in some way selfish are the people who have been benefiting from us having none.

Boundaries are, in fact, helpful, for others as well as for us, as they provide others with a clearer understanding of what matters to us, who we are, and where our limits lie. Saying yes to almost everything might feel good in the moment, but when we find ourselves overloaded with other obligations and unable to keep our commitments, we can end up disappointing both ourselves and others. And we can even begin to feel resentful and annoyed for having been asked to do things in the first place.

Although saying no to invites and requests might therefore feel disappointing in the moment, down the line it can really serve people better as, in this way, we are left with both a clear conscience and a full tank of gas.

Sometimes, the most loving gesture is to say no.

Misconception 3: Boundaries Are Telling Someone Else What to Do

We can make healthy boundary requests in any relationship. But let's be clear that *asking* for a change and *demanding* a change, or telling someone what to do, are by no means the same thing. By extension then, it really is a misconception that boundaries are in any way bossy or demanding.

For example, we can request that a sibling starts going to therapy, and hope that they comply, but we cannot demand or expect it of them. As in any respectful adult-to-adult relationship, the other person then has the right to say yes, no, or propose a compromise in response.

Communicating boundaries to other people means communicating limits that you have, asking them to respect these limits, and making it clear what you will do if they deny your requests. For example, a boundary statement might sound like "If you continue to speak about our parents in this way, I'm going to draw a line under that topic of conversation" or "If you continue to speak to me in that way, I will leave the room."

Beware, however, of boundaries that tap into, or prey on, the fears of another, as these can quickly become a subtle form of manipulation. Unlike manipulation, healthy boundary setting isn't about gaining control or power over another; it's about making choices about our *own* behavior and our *own* life. As such, boundaries move the focus of control to where we actually have control, which is within our own actions. So it is important to understand this distinction.

Misconception 4: Boundaries Aren't for Families

Families are complex systems where boundaries are often very much needed. Yet one of the more worrisome myths around family is that we have to simply put up with unkind words and behaviors from certain people just because "they're family."

Family is not a free pass for disrespectful or abusive behavior. If we wouldn't accept similar behavior from outside the immediate family, why would we allow it from our siblings, our parents, or other relatives?

Many people are raised to respect the family unit, and this may have required them having to bite their tongue about certain things, accepting another's behavior as "just the way they are," or walking on eggshells in an attempt to keep a semblance of harmony. However, boundaries are necessary even in the most well-functioning of family relationships. Setting boundaries will support you as you grow both within and beyond the family unit, and will also allow you to move away from the expectations of others.

KNOWING OUR RELATIONSHIP WITH BOUNDARIES

Boundaries are central to any relationship, with some being deeply complex, while others are more straightforward; and some being difficult to hear, while others being difficult to apply and honor.

Before we look at ways to establish boundaries, remind yourself that there is no need to ever feel guilty, ashamed, or selfish for creating boundaries.

By forming boundaries, you are choosing:

* Temporary discomfort over long-term resentment
* Self-respect over self-sabotage
* Well-being over burnout
* Authentic connection over staying "hidden" behind the mask of people pleasing

FAMILY
IS NOT A
JUSTIFICATION,
NOR AN EXCUSE,
FOR HARMFUL
BEHAVIOR

SETTING BOUNDARIES

Boundaries are deeply personal, so vary vastly from one person to the next. They also change throughout the course of people's lives. While there is no "one way" to navigate boundary-setting, I hope that the following steps might be a helpful starting point:

1. Identify Your Limits

It goes without saying that we can't set good boundaries if we're unsure of what we want them to be. This can be a difficult hurdle for many to overcome, particularly if we didn't have healthy boundary behaviors modeled for us as children. Subsequently, many of us won't know that a boundary, or limit, has been crossed until we begin to feel out of sorts, or "dysregulated," in some form.

A good way to identify a limit is to consider past experiences where you have felt frustration, resentment, discomfort, or defensiveness about a line having been crossed. How did your body feel when this happened? Did you have a racing heart? A flushed face? Were you trembling? Consider in light of this what you can accept and what makes you feel too uncomfortable to accept. What are you willing to tolerate and what is a hard no? Learning to tune into the messages you receive from your body and mind will help you identify what your limits are.

2. Consider the Consequence

In boundary formation, a consequence is the action you are willing to take if or when your boundary is crossed by another. Once you have decided on a boundary, it can be useful to write down some rough drafts of wording for it, complete with a consequence, or consequences, embedded within. This should make it clear what will happen if the boundary isn't respected.

One of the most underrated ways that we can love someone is to uphold our word, including following through on what we claim will happen if a boundary is crossed. So while honoring our own boundaries may feel harsh, it can actually help relationships thrive as it will prevent us from living in the shadow of resentment, passive aggression, or animosity in the long term.

Examples of boundary statements, complete with consequences, include:

* I feel uncomfortable when you speak badly about other people in front of me. If this keeps happening, I will have to leave early.
* If you continue to speak to me in that way, I will have to hang up the phone.
* If you keep ignoring what I'm saying, I will assume you're not interested in spending quality time together and I will go home.
* When you cancel our plans at the last minute, I am left holding how hurt and disappointed I am with your decision. In future, I will communicate with you how this makes me feel so that I don't carry the load alone.

* I am open to discussing a solution with you. I am not open to debating my feelings. If you're unable to discuss solutions at this point, let's take some time out to cool down.

Consequences are about letting the other person know what will happen if they cross your limit. It is best to avoid harsh ultimatums but to be honest with what actions you are willing to take. It is also best to allow for incremental change—the cost of a crossed boundary doesn't have to be set in stone, but it does need to be clear.

A lot of people get stuck trying to find a way around having to communicate a boundary or set a consequence. As a result, they might, for example, end up spending energy trying to make our limits overly palatable to others, with the resulting boundary falling short of where it needs to be. It's best to be gracious but firm when establishing your consequence; we love not just through speech, but through action.

3. Communicate the Boundary

Knowing what you want your boundary to be is great, but this is of little use if we don't follow through by communicating this to others or if we fall into the thinking trap of "I shouldn't have to say it. They should just know."

Like any new skill, communicating boundaries takes practice. Being clear and assertive can be scary, so start small with people you don't know and build up your skills from there. For example, if there's been a mistake with your food order, communicate this in a firm but friendly way to the waiter. If an acquaintance asks you

something private that you'd rather not speak about, say no. If you're overcharged, communicate this with the cashier. If you're messaged on Instagram by someone telling you to invest in an up-and-coming stock or who says "Hey baby. Let's chat," block them. These small interactions with strangers, where the risks feel small, are great ways of building up our assertive abilities.

As we then increase our level of comfort with speaking up, we can begin to put our growing assertiveness into practice with those in our inner circle. The key to communicating our boundaries with family and friends is being clear and direct but respectful.

"No" is a complete sentence and yet when it comes to those close to us, sometimes we may want to offer more of an explanation; not always, but sometimes. Be mindful not to fall into justification where it's not necessary. Say as little or as much as you are comfortable saying without sinking into any kind of negative tone.

Using "I" statements can be helpful for this, such as "I feel sad when you dismiss me. If this continues to happen, I will gently alert you to it. And if it doesn't change, I will leave the room. What I need is for you to let me know that you are listening and that you hear me." Statements like this help to convey both confidence and self-respect.

Communicating your boundaries to others will make them feel safe to communicate their boundaries with you, too. If it feels safe to do so, you might want to consider discussing this section of the book with a close friend and see what boundaries you can come up with, together.

Take 5: Create Your Own
"I"-Statement Boundary

Use the below wording to form a boundary statement of your own that you can work toward implementing:

* I feel [emotion] when you [behavior].
* If this continues to happen, I will [consequence].
* What I need is [need].

4. Uphold the Boundary

The final phase of honoring, or upholding, your boundaries is often the most challenging as it requires both strength and consistency when people test our resolve.

At the end of the day, boundaries that we set *will* be tried and tested. Even after we have communicated both the boundaries and the consequences of crossing them, there will be some people in our lives who will continually attempt to push back, whether consciously or not.

It's normal to experience some level of push-back, especially from those who have grown accustomed to our previous lack of boundaries. The trick is to *anticipate* the push-back and simply take it as a test that enables you to reinforce your limits. Your self-esteem and self-regard will thank you for it in the end.

Going back to our earlier door analogy, the people arriving at your front door will continue to walk in as they wish until they see that the door really is closed. Every time we go back on our boundaries by leaving the door open, we're giving others permission to get their own way again, because if *we* don't honor our own boundaries, why would they?

The good news is that every time you uphold a boundary, you have the opportunity to alter other people's expectations of you as well as to increase your own level of self-trust.

Common responses of loved ones to new boundaries that we set often include:

* "You've changed."
* "I miss the old you."
* "You're too sensitive now."
* "You're being really selfish."
* "I'm disappointed in you."
* "Someone's been watching too much TV."

If certain people continue to push against your communicated boundaries, recognize that although we cannot change people, we can change how we relate to certain people. In some cases, it may therefore be time to reassess what you define as the consequence of crossing your boundaries.

Sometimes, such as with someone who repeatedly disrespects your limits, this might involve taking a break from the relationship for a period of time, or even for good. Defining and asserting our boundaries can be deeply complex, particularly with family and loved ones, so if you're really struggling with it, do reach out for support.

Having a trusted friend as a source of gentle guidance or as a sounding board can sometimes really help you to unpick the knots of complex situations. Otherwise, if you feel you need more support than this, do consider reaching out to a mental health professional.

When sticking to your boundaries starts to get tough, it's important to remember why you set them in the first place. Remind yourself that you need them for your wellbeing, and that you need this, no matter what others may say.

Boundaries aren't just a sign of healthy relationships with others; they're also a sign of a healthy relationship with yourself—self-respect, self-worth, and genuine self-care.

Sometimes, the onus falls on us to set the ultimate consequence—walking away and choosing a healthier path. Nothing communicates your boundaries better than living by them.

Take 5: Honor Your Boundaries

Boundaries are all about honing in on your feelings and honoring them. If you notice you're consistently not sustaining your own boundaries, or if another person is continually crossing them, ask yourself:

* What am I/is this person doing?

* What am I going to do about this situation?

* What do I have control of?

CHANGING BOUNDARIES

Boundaries can change. As time passes and we continue to work on ourselves, we will see whether certain boundaries serve or hinder us. Nine times out of ten, they will need to change as we continue to work at healing wounds that our boundaries are supporting us with. But just because you've outgrown a boundary, it doesn't mean it wasn't right at the time.

Likewise, boundaries that feel right for one relationship may not fit another. Certain situations and relationships, such as those with difficult family members or challenging colleagues, are likely to call for stricter, more rigid boundaries. In the meantime, you may feel that other relationships, such as with your best friend, can have more softness and flexibility. Just take time to discover what feels right for you.

As we learn more about ourselves and start to integrate more self-regulation practices into our daily lives (see Chapter 5), we may find that we can engage better with our own needs and boundaries without feeling overwhelmed or frozen.

It's key to allow yourself time before changing your boundaries, particularly with any experience of trauma. You are doing the very best for you by giving yourself permission to go slowly. Trying to heal too quickly is a disaster waiting stage left. Always prioritize safety first and foremost.

Over time, we may consider softening our boundaries when someone has been consistently respectful of our limits and our vulnerabilities—as a sign of our trust in them. It may also be worth considering softening them if we're feeling increasingly disconnected from people we care for and trust—especially if we've come to realize that in trying to create a secure "front door," we've actually created an enormous brick wall!

Take your time and exercise discernment as you continue to grow and change, day by day, moment by moment.

FINDING THE LANGUAGE FOR OUR BOUNDARIES

Sometimes boundary-setting can be in the form of simple statements; other times it may require more of a discussion.

In the pages that follow, you will find examples of boundary statements relating to different situations, such as for occasions and holidays, for use with family and friends, for use with partners, and for use during conflict.

As you read through the example statements, they may sound a bit alien or formal to you in many cases. So please know that they are only meant as rough starting points or guides. Ultimately it is up to each of us, as individuals, to establish content and wordings that will work for us.

As you explore the examples, feel free to rewrite any that appeal to you in your own vernacular, and try speaking them aloud to get used to hearing them in your own voice and to see how they feel.

Boundaries for Occasions and Holidays

At the height of the holiday season, there are often a bunch of commitments and invitations. Perhaps they're already behind you and you're feeling the need for some down time and rest. Or perhaps you're still trying to juggle them. Either way, busy times like this, where there are a plethora of events and gatherings, can really test our boundaries.

Might any of the following statements fit your situation and resonate with you? If so, feel free to rework them into your own personal wordings:

* Thanks for inviting me. Just a heads-up—I will only be able to stay until 8:30 p.m.
* This sounds like something you need to discuss with [person]. I am not getting involved in this.
* I want to spend time with you, but if you continue to speak about [topic] in that way, I will leave.
* I'm not comfortable speaking about that. Can we change the subject?
* I won't be able to stay the night, but I'm really looking forward to spending time with you.
* I can't right now. I am going to go to my room to get in some quiet time.
* No thanks, I've had enough to drink.
* I would love to catch up. It's too late now but how about [day/time] instead?

Boundaries with Family and Friends

Setting boundaries with those closest to us are some of the trickiest limits we can implement and hold. Our inner circle has a unique way of shedding light on the unhealed, unconscious parts of ourselves. However, setting good boundaries should help to protect both you and those around you from lots of unnecessary frustration, confusion, and anxiety.

Might any of the following statements fit your situation and resonate with you? If so, feel free to rework them into your own personal wordings:

* I appreciate that but I'd like to try taking care of this by myself. I will let you know if I need some help.
* I feel uncomfortable when you speak about [topic]. I would like to speak about something else.
* I am not looking for advice. If you can right now, I would really like you to listen.
* I'd love to catch up with you but I also need to rest for work the next day. Let's agree on a time that suits us both. After [time] doesn't work for me.
* I love talking to you but I'm finding I don't have the time to speak every day. Can we agree to talk every [particular day] and [particular day]?
* I understand you're frustrated, but I'm not willing to listen to you speak about [person] in this way.
* I know you care, but we are choosing to parent in a way that suits us both. I would like you to respect that.
* I understand where you're coming from, but I need to make decisions that work for me. If you can respect that, I can speak about this further with you.

Boundaries with Partners

Having boundaries in place with your girlfriend, boyfriend, partner, wife, husband, or significant other will help you define what you are comfortable with and how you would like to be treated.

Talking about boundaries can happen whenever and wherever. A simple "I really like it when you…" or "I'm not comfortable when we…" can be a simple way of opening up a dialogue around boundaries.

In healthy relationships, partners generally respect the boundaries of the other but we're all human, so we will all slip up at times and overstep the mark. It's important to take such slip-ups as opportunities to have open, honest discussions where we apologize and reset things.

If you feel afraid about talking boundaries with your partner in case they might react with anger or violence, be mindful that this could be a sign that the relationship may be in some way abusive. If you feel this may be the case, please do consider seeking the comfort of a trusted friend and/or a mental health professional.

If, however, you feel comfortable talking to your partner, might any of the following statements fit your situation and resonate with you? If so, feel free to rework them into your own personal wordings:

* I am happy for us to follow each other on social media, but I am not comfortable with a joint profile/sharing my passwords with you.
* I love kissing you but I would like to take it down a notch in public. Can we discuss this?

* I like catching up with you during the day, but I can't text multiple times an hour. If you text me, I will be able to get back to you on my break and/or when I've finished work.
* I love living together but I also need time by myself. Can we talk about a way we can facilitate this?
* I'm feeling really tired today. Could you take care of dinner later?
* When I get home from work, I would like to unwind for half an hour before we talk about our day. Could we agree to try this?
* I would love to spend some quality time with you without our phones in the evening. Can we discuss a time that we could agree to put them away?
* I love having the weekends together, but I would also like to have some time to meet up with friends and family. Let's talk about how we could balance this.

Boundaries During Conflict

During moments of conflict, when the emotional temperature of a situation shoots up and we become out of sorts and dysregulated, we're liable to accidentally revert to old patterns of communication. It becomes more important than ever during such times to really listen and be heard; to see and be seen; to pause and acknowledge.

Creating boundaries about the way you approach and resolve conflict is perhaps one of the most important conversations a couple can have. However, the example boundaries listed below can be applied across the board in terms of relationships in your life.

Might any of the following statements fit your situation and resonate with you? If so, feel free to rework them into your own personal wordings:

* I need to take some space right now so that we can continue to communicate effectively. I'll come back in twenty minutes.
* I would like us to take time out from this conversation and hold hands for a bit.
* I'm feeling a bit floaty. Can you bring down your volume please?
* I'm not sure I understand what you're saying. Can you rephrase it so I can understand it better?
* I understand you're angry right now, but it is not OK to speak to me in that way. If you continue, I will leave the room.
* If you continue to punish yourself and me in this way, I will have to consider all of my options going forward, including leaving this relationship.
* I appreciate that you're feeling frustrated, but please do not criticize me in that way. It's hurtful, disrespectful, and it's distracting from what this is really about.
* We keep going back to this point without making any progress toward a solution. Can we take some time to think about what really needs to be addressed?
* I don't feel heard. I would like you to acknowledge what I am saying before we continue.

BOUNDARIES WITH YOURSELF

Boundaries are not just for our relationships with others; we also need them with ourselves. They help us to monitor our behavior and make choices that serve our best interests, even if they feel hard to put into action.

It is likely to be particularly difficult to set boundaries with ourselves if our caregivers didn't model healthy limits in this regard and/or were inconsistent with their reactions and rules.

If boundaries were either absent or excessively harsh from an early age, as an adult, we can then feel that boundaries are either controlling us or depriving us of something. Outside of this, certain mental health issues and addictions can make it feel nearly impossible to apply self-boundaries.

There are many reasons why creating boundaries for ourselves can be a struggle but, ultimately, setting positive self-boundaries will give you a sense of safety and structure—the groundwork for healthy "reparenting," which we'll explore in Chapter 7.

Examples of boundaries for the self include:

* Brushing your teeth twice a day
* Listening to one podcast a day
* Limiting your daily scroll time
* Having no more than two cups of coffee a day
* Limiting your alcohol intake to one day a week
* Stepping away from the mirror
* Leaving work emails untouched over the weekend
* Opting out of gossip
* Washing your face before you go to bed
* Keeping to a regular bedtime routine.

Small incremental change is key here. Expecting perfection is counterproductive so be gentle with your learning process. Nothing but resentment and shame come from being too harsh or unrealistic. Reflect on the reasons you're slipping up as and when this happens, and aim to address what you need to with curiosity and compassion.

Setting boundaries with both others and ourselves is a skill that takes courage and communication—and one that you can only hone and polish through practice. So keep practicing…

THE FOUR PILLARS OF ADDRESSING A CROSSED BOUNDARY

Love is easy. Relationships are difficult. And when a boundary is crossed with a partner, friends, or a family member, it can slowly chip away at the health of the relationship if left to fester. More often than not, people will cross our boundaries without realizing and without intention, but whether it's conscious or not, the end result is the same. It's important that when a boundary is crossed, we deal with it in a way that's reparative and constructive. This is how to do it:

1. Recognize

Notice what happens within you when you recognize that a boundary you have set has been crossed. Before naming the emotions at play, observe the feelings in your body. How does your chest feel? How does your stomach feel? Perhaps your hands feel cold? Or you're awash with heat? What thoughts are emerging? Maybe things like "They don't respect me," "I'm just a nag," or "Nobody listens to me"? Practice holding each of these thoughts tentatively and with interest. When you have gathered the signals from your body and mind, start to identify and name the emotions present. Observing and collecting all the information in this way will help to inform what it is you wish to communicate to others about your boundaries later.

2. Regulate

After becoming aware of the messages from the mind and body, take a moment to pause and breathe deeply. Creating space between the reaction (those reflex thoughts and behaviors), and the response (how we wish to communicate in the situation) is integral to understanding what's happening within you, and to being able to communicate that effectively.

How many times in the past have you jumped straight out of the gate, only to later regret what you said or feel angry at yourself for not having said something else? As annoying, uncomfortable, and upsetting as it can be, someone crossing a boundary of yours almost always provides you with an opportunity to learn about yourself. So, if you can, take some time to either walk with your reaction, sit and journal with it, or just take some deep breaths around it—to regulate your emotions as best you can, and to see what emerges from this space.

3. Reinstate

Next, it's important to take time to acknowledge how your boundary has been violated and what boundary you will now need to reinstate.

When doing this, it is important to consider what you will do and say when this newly instated boundary is next crossed. Within client work, I will often hear, "Well, I've said it now. So hopefully they won't do that again." It falls to me to ask, "When they *do*, how would you like to respond?" As much as we would love a boundary to automatically be upheld and respected after one conversation, examples of this are the exception as opposed to the rule.

In some cases, the crossing of your boundary may even be a kind of test for you at the hands of friends or family, whether intentional or unintentional.

It's therefore good practice to accept that you will have to reinstate boundaries again down the line, as they will be crossed at some point again. This way, you will be prepared for, rather than surprised by, the overstep, and you will feel more comfortable to speak up.

After all, if you don't speak up when something's bothering you, you can't ever expect change. Humans are habitual creatures, so boundaries are likely to have to be reinstated twice, three times, maybe more. It's up to you how many times you feel comfortable reinstating your boundaries. But if they are regularly overlooked and violated, it may be worth moving to the next step of "reconsidering" certain relationships once it gets to a certain point…

4. Reconsider

If a boundary of yours is consistently being disregarded after clear communication, it may be time to re-evaluate, or "reconsider," the relationship with the person doing the disrespecting, as well as the amount of time and energy this person receives from you.

The key to boundaries is respect for yourself as well as for others. You are the only person who can advocate for yourself, so if someone is repeatedly making you feel uncomfortable, it is not selfish to reconsider how much of your life they deserve access to. This includes family.

This can be especially challenging if you are living with the person, you deeply care for them, or if they are in a position of authority. We have to identify what choices we have and choose the best option for ourselves in the moment, showing ourselves respect and trusting our gut.

Such choices are unlikely to be easy. They may involve all sorts of upheavals. But life is complicated, and boundary violations sometimes involve making difficult decisions. However, please don't feel that you have to go through the process alone. Always know that you can seek the support of someone safe to help you to find and do what is best for you, whether a trusted friend or a mental health professional.

REPAIRING OUR OWN BOUNDARY TRANSGRESSIONS

While we're talking about boundaries being crossed, it's important to address how we might "repair" any boundary transgressions of our own, whether intentional or not. When we cross the boundary of another, the possibility for reparation tends to lie in two main actions:

1. Offering a genuine apology
2. Engaging in open discussion

IF SOMEONE
CONTINUES TO PUSH
AGAINST YOUR
BOUNDARIES,
RECOGNIZE THAT
YOU CANNOT CHANGE
SOMEONE, BUT YOU CAN
CHANGE HOW YOU
RELATE TO SOMEONE

Offering a Genuine Apology

Most of us will have experienced at some point in our lives the frustration of receiving a "non-apology"—a rejection of personal responsibility wrapped up in apology wording.

Examples of such "non-apologies" can include:

* "I'm sorry you feel that way!"
* "I'm sorry BUT ..."
* "I didn't mean it!"
* "I'm only human!"
* "I'm the worst."
* "I'm sorry I said that—you provoked me!"
* "I'm just tired and having a bad day."

In contrast to this, a genuine, heartfelt apology—whether in relation to boundaries or anything else—should:

* Acknowledge why the other person was hurt
* Take ownership of personal behavior
* Accept responsibility rather than project and reject it
* Not be backed up with a defense or justification
* Not make the other person feel worse.

Quite often when someone is expressing anger, it is because they have been hurt, such as by having had key boundaries of theirs transgressed.

In such cases, it is this person's responsibility to acknowledge the hurt and to communicate it in a way that is respectful. If they choose to do this, we have a chance to offer a genuine apology for whatever has happened.

Remember: a pseudo-apology, or "non-apology" (like the ones listed opposite), will offer them little solace, and do little more than provide us with insulation from a healthy dose of shame, so it's important to ensure that you are as open, honest, genuine, brave, and vulnerable as possible in your apology.

Apologizing doesn't, however, mean berating ourselves or allowing ourselves to be paralyzed with guilt. A light, fleeting sense of shame can help to bring us back to center; it is natural and even good to feel a bit bad for hurting someone. It means you care, and an apology has the power to connect you with the person who has been hurt.

Rather than viewing a heartfelt apology as any sort of weakness, it's important to recognize it as both a humble and noble act, with the power to help heal wounds, both old and new. It is therefore always worth offering a true apology from the heart.

Engaging in Open Discussion

Every person is different, so will have different boundaries. If in doubt as to what someone's boundaries are or as to whether you have crossed them, just ask. Not everyone will be happy to broach a conversation about this topic, but this doesn't necessarily mean that they wouldn't be open to taking part in a conversation if you initiate it.

Initiating a discussion can save you a lot of mental energy instead of entering into a cognitive and emotional tug of war where you try to decipher the unspoken limits of another.

As you get to discuss things and know a person better, you will begin to get a better sense of their boundaries and what they mean to them. As you do, you will undoubtedly discover that areas of your boundaries clash. Facilitating an open discussion around this and coming to a solution that would work for both of you, rather than just one of you, will benefit the relationship equally.

Although some boundaries will be difficult to discuss, and some issues may be difficult to "repair," risking vulnerability by opening a dialogue early on will be likely to save you a lot of pain in the long run.

MENTAL NOTES

Take five minutes at the end of each day for a month to reflect on the following:

* What would it have felt freeing to say "No" or "Yes" to today?
  (E.g. No to weekend plans, Yes to support on a project.)

* What boundaries are helping/would help support me right now? (E.g. The time
  limit I've placed on social media.)

* If I was already living according to healthy boundaries, how would it feel? Write
  your answer in the present tense. (E.g. I feel empowered. I feel confident. I feel
  joyful. I feel steady.)

* What affirmation can I offer myself to help me respect my own boundaries
  more going forward? (E.g. I am deserving of setting boundaries that serve me; I
  take care of myself and my relationships by honoring my boundaries; see page
  115 if you'd like any help in creating your own affirmation.)

By the end of the month, you'll have collected reams of helpful information about
your approach to boundaries in life, including ideas of how you can move forward as
positively as possible with this for optimal self-care.

7.
Reparenting

HOW TO HEAL
YOURSELF

"If you think you're enlightened, go spend a week with your family."
Ram Dass

Traditionally, "reparenting" was a term used for when, within the context of a therapeutic relationship, a therapist would play the role of a parent to a client who had experienced dysfunctional or abusive treatment as they were growing up.

But as we've continued to grow more conscious as a society, the process of reparenting has become increasingly accessible beyond the four walls of the therapy room. The term is therefore now used to refer to individuals making the conscious decision to be kind, loving parents to *themselves* in order to heal any wounds that their inner child might still be carrying—a process that is sometimes also called self-parenting, or self-reparenting.

WHAT DO WE MEAN BY OUR "INNER CHILD?"

You may have heard the term "inner child," rolled your eyes, and thought "what a load of waffle." I understand if so, as such terms are often bandied around so much these days that they can begin to sound clichéd. But my hope is that some unpacking around the term will help to clarify its relevance to us all.

Each of us has been influenced by our environment from birth—shaped through the significant people around us and the events that we have lived through. As children, we absorb a great deal from our friends, families, teachers, caregivers, and all others who we encounter. And even though we don't consciously acknowledge, or even remember, everything that we experience, we log these experiences in our unconscious mind and in our bodies.

Many of these unconscious imprints often live on within us as adults—as part of our inner child whose early wounds have yet to be healed and who therefore wants to be seen, heard, and unconditionally loved. As such, the inner child present within each of us today is the echo of the child we once were—and is often in need of our care and compassion.

WHAT DOES REPARENTING INVOLVE?

Reparenting involves us going inward to explore the previously unmet needs, worries, memories, and stories of our inner child from the place of maturity that we are now in, as adults. The reason for doing this is to give our inner child different perspectives than the ones it originally experienced, therefore allowing us to start responding in more helpful ways to any triggers that emerge in our current lives (see Chapter 4 for a reminder of how triggers work).

Reparenting is a parallel journey of learning and unlearning. We must learn what we needed (and weren't given) as a child—and how to provide this for ourselves today. And to do this, we must unlearn any limiting thoughts, feelings, and beliefs that were unconsciously formed in our early years around the notions of safety, love, and self-worth.

Although it can be useful to undertake this journey with the guidance of a qualified therapist, we each have the capacity to at least start this reparenting journey ourselves if we feel so inclined.

WHY REPARENT OURSELVES?

When deep needs go unmet at an early age, or we undergo trauma, an unconscious part of ourselves can get stuck in those moments of development, leaving us unable, even in adulthood, to move past whatever beliefs and patterns formed around these incidents at the time.

When this happens, even though we can appear to be fully functional adults on the outside, our inner child is often still scared and struggling on the inside, using a lot of energy trying to deal with our past experiences.

So, for example, if the young, vulnerable part of us is triggered in some way in adult life, such as by a certain tone of voice that reminds us of something in our childhood, we are likely to react from the wound created back at that time, with all of the insight and wisdom that we had at that moment in our timeline—which, more often than not, wasn't all that much given our tender age!

We might, for example, therefore find ourselves being as nice as possible to a person talking to us angrily in order to try to stop their anger from growing, or we might find ourselves withdrawing from an awkward situation altogether in order to "disappear" and protect ourselves, rather than feeling empowered enough to speak up against something that is making us feel uncomfortable.

By learning how to reparent ourselves, we give our inner child what it needs to feel safe and loved in the here and now, thus breaking the need to continue the old patterns of, for example, being nice to someone abusing us or not feeling that it's safe for us to speak up. In so doing, this part of our inner child can start to relax and become integrated into the conscious, confident person that we're becoming today.

In short then: by reparenting, we start to repattern. And, as such, reparenting is a powerfully healing process for most people.

It's important to remember that we're all imperfect humans raised by imperfect humans. The process of reparenting is therefore in no way an exercise in finger-pointing or blaming our past or our caregivers.

Instead, reparenting is a means to:

* Understand and validate the experiences that we have lived through
* Heal wounds created early in life that we may still be carrying with us today (however small)
* Move beyond any limiting beliefs that were formed in our early years
* Create new patterns of thought and behavior that allow us to move forward feeling happier and healthier.

You are likely to benefit from going on a journey of reparenting if:

* You recognize unhealthy patterns in your relationships
* You grew up in a volatile environment
* A caregiver was neglectful, abusive, or absent during your childhood
* You have a hard time creating and keeping boundaries
* You could be described as a "people-pleaser"
* You place your self-worth on the opinions of others
* You believe self-care is indulgent
* You struggle with negative self-talk
* You have a difficult time making decisions out of fear of disappointing others.

GETTING TO KNOW OUR INNER PARENT

Whether we're conscious of it or not, we are all already a parent to ourselves in many ways—in that we're responsible for meeting our own needs. For some, I understand this statement may feel a little strange. So let's look at a few examples of how this plays itself out.

When you're hungry, who buys and/or makes food for you? When you need a new coat, who goes out and gets you one? When you feel sad, who, without fail, will sit with you until it passes? The answer to all of these is, of course, you (albeit that you might have a partner, friends, or family who help with such things, too).

THE BELIEFS +
PATTERNS WE DEVELOP
IN CHILDHOOD STAY
WITHIN—
UNTIL WE BEGIN
TO QUESTION
THEM

We are, however, more often than not unaware of this parenting role that we play for ourselves. And, as such, we also tend to be unaware of the type of parent we are being to ourselves.

Unfortunately, the tendency when we're operating from such a lack of awareness is to echo qualities of our original caregivers and/or to reinforce unconscious beliefs that formed when we were young, which may not have been ideal.

The trick to reparenting is therefore to become aware of our role as a parent to our inner child and to actively decide, based on the needs of this inner child, what kind of parent we want to be.

Take 5: Assess Your Inner Parent

To establish what type of parent you're currently being to yourself, take a few moments to ask yourself the following questions:

* Am I kind, compassionate, and supportive of my inner child? Do I talk kindly to myself and celebrate myself as well as tending to my most fundamental needs?
* Or am I a harsh, critical parent? Or potentially even an absent parent? Maybe dismissing my own needs, focusing more on the negative than the positive, and/or discouraging the expression of emotions?

Whatever the answers, is this the type of parent that I would like to be to myself moving forward?

THE FISHBOWL ANALOGY

In the pages that follow you will find suggestions on how to begin your journey of conscious reparenting. But it might be useful for you to first visualize a goldfish bowl filled with water, and a fish swimming in it. The fish represents the adult that you are today, and the pool of water your early childhood experiences.

Inevitably, the water will have accumulated some unhealthy grime during the time you've been swimming in it and, depending on the nature of your early experiences, the water may be pretty sludgy by this stage.

Now visualize sieving all the grit and grime out from the water, until you are left with nice clear water in its place (the cleaning process represents you establishing new healthy reparenting habits with your inner child).

By doing this, you not only make the water clearer; you also become more aware of the importance of the water quality so that you won't allow the grime to build up in the same way again—whether by bringing it in yourself or by allowing other people to plonk their sludge into your bowl.

This fishbowl analogy is a visual reminder that the early memories we store can, after a while, start to impact us as adults but that we can choose to clean out our fishbowl at any time we want—to enable the fish to swim more freely and easily again (i.e. to enable our adult self to go about our daily business with more ease and contentment again!).

Take 5: Clean Out Your Fishbowl

Take a moment to consider the water in your own fishbowl. What does it look like? And what does it feel like to swim in? Ask yourself questions such as:

Have I done, or am I doing, anything that is making the water dirtier?

What have I allowed other people to add to the water?

What small things would help me make the water clearer moving forward?

Before we get started, please note:

* Reparenting is a slow, ongoing process, but one that holds benefits for anyone who embarks on it. Patience and compassion will be two of your best allies.
* You are likely to make mistakes along the way so make peace with that now. It's OK. It isn't about the rupture; it's about the repair.
* Reparenting can be a challenging journey. If possible, consider embarking on it with a qualified therapist.
* It's OK if now isn't the right time for you to start. Read through the material and know that guidance is here if and when you need it.

WAYS TO CONNECT WITH OUR INNER CHILD

Some of the key ways that we can connect with our inner child (or clean out the water in our fishbowl) are:

* Visual recall
* Reintroduce play!
* Write a letter to your inner child
* Speak kindly to yourself

We will explore each of these in turn in a moment ...

However, it's important to firstly remember that the work of connecting to your inner child can be challenging for both your mind and body. So I cannot emphasize enough how important it is to undertake the process slowly and with care.

Be sure to check in with yourself regularly by asking questions like: Do I have the energy to engage with this right now? How does my body feel? What is my intention? Do I have the space to hold whatever may come with kindness right now?

Only proceed when you feel sure that you have the space and capacity to provide yourself with all the love and kindness you need. And each time that you finish one of the inner child connection exercises in the pages that follow, visualize placing your inner child back inside the warmth and care of your gentle heart so that you never leave it exposed as you resume your normal everyday activities.

Visual Recall

One effective way to connect with your inner child is to "time-travel" back to infanthood using a photograph of your younger self as inspiration:

1. Find a photograph, or several photographs, of yourself as a baby, toddler, and/or young child.
2. Spend some quiet time just looking at the photo(s) to rediscover what your younger self looked like.
3. Tune in with what is coming up for you as you look at the photograph(s). For example, what physical sensations are occurring? And what emotions are you feeling? This work can be difficult for many, so take your time. Keep in mind that it is often easier for us to feel compassion for others than it is ourselves. After all, we may have rejected or ignored our inner child for a long time.
4. Just allow whatever feelings that come up to be present without criticizing or rejecting them. We don't have to fully understand each one or why it is appearing. Simply aim to handle each one with care and kindness.

The aim here is to recognize on some level that, no matter what comes up, we can allow it to just be and continue to show our inner child the compassion that it so longs for.

Reintroduce Play!

Making time to include activities in your adult life that you loved to do as a child is one of the most overlooked avenues of healing available to us. When we create time in our lives to facilitate a form of play, or activity, that our younger self loved, our inner child is seen, heard, and validated. Play is as important in our adult life as it was in childhood:

1. Find a comfortable place to sit with a notepad and pen, and think about what brought you joy as a child.
2. Allow yourself to fall into memories and daydreams as you consider: What did I love doing? Your answers might include anything from reading books, watching movies, playing certain sports or games, playing with particular toys, spending time with certain people or animals, learning about particular subjects or eating certain foods…
3. Be both as general and as specific as you can, jotting down anything that comes to mind and allowing the list to flow across the page.
4. From the list, then pick out one thing that you would like to "re-create," or reinject into your life again. For example, if you loved swimming, might you be able to do that this week? If you loved climbing trees, is there a climbing center near you that you could visit? If you loved painting, could you make time for this again or join a local class? "Re-creating" might look like going to the seaside to build a sandcastle to one person; singing at the top of your lungs for another; starting arts and crafts again for another; having a dance party in your bedroom; rereading the Harry Potters (or whatever your

favorite childhood book was); or anything else thoroughly enjoyable that springs to mind.

5. Note that you might initially find yourself having objections to bringing more play back into your life, such as "I can't do that," "I have responsibilities," or "I don't have time." But be sure to move beyond any such objections.

6. Tune in with what comes up as you then re-create your act of joyful play for your inner child and journal about the experience after. Use this writing time to explore any embarrassment or silliness you felt, or feel, toward the idea. It's normal to feel a bit self-conscious or foolish in the beginning. Go forward anyway and keep an open mind.

Write a Letter to Your Inner Child

If you could spend a moment with your four-year-old self, what would you say? How about your eight-year-old or twelve-year-old self? Acknowledging and interacting with your inner child through the process of letter-writing is a powerful way to connect with the younger you:

1. Get a pen and paper, and find a quiet, comfortable place where you feel safe to be open.

2. Take a few moments to ground yourself, visualizing yourself as the kind, gentle parent you needed as a child, and letting the love and compassion you have for your inner child flow freely.

3. Now write a letter that will make the young you feel safe and loved. This may involve recalling a happy memory; it may include an apology; it may look more like a promise; or it may be a simple declaration of wanting to build a stronger connection with your inner child. There is no right or wrong here, and no one will be judging you.

4. As you write, ask your inner child what they are feeling and what they need right now, and allow your writing to be guided by this. If you feel emotional during the process, it's OK. Just allow any tears to be present without shame; instead, be proud of the courage you have to express them and of the affirming and gentle parent you are becoming to yourself.

After you've written this initial letter to your inner child, you might find yourself wanting to write several more over the next few days or few weeks. Please do so if this feels right.

You might then even find that your inner child wants to write back, as they have things they want to say or questions to ask. So honor this if the urge emerges. Using your non-dominant hand to write this can assist in bypassing the logical side of the brain to get more in touch with what your inner child is really feeling. Consider exploring things such as whether, as a child, you were ever met with frustration and annoyance for certain behaviors, and express how this made you feel.

If so, then, in any further letters that you write in response to your inner child, be sure to offer your younger self the patience, space, love, and kindness that they need around this.

By creating a pen-pal dialogue with your inner child, you create a space in which healing and transformation can effectively occur.

Speak Kindly to Yourself

Children often believe that they must earn love through acquiring certain grades or behaving in certain ways. We may not have had parents who told us that we deserved love, no matter what we achieved or how we behaved.

As devastating as this can be on the child we were and the adult we now are, we have the chance, as adults, to offer ourselves the words that we so desperately needed to hear when we were young. There are many things that our inner child may need to hear in a calm, soothing tone from a gentle parent.

Nurturing words that you might want to offer your inner child include:

* "I love you"
* "You are protected"
* "I'm sorry"
* "Thank you"
* "It's good to play"
* "You are safe"
* "I hear you and I am proud of you"
* "It's OK to feel this emotion"
* "You didn't deserve what happened to you"
* "You are enough. You are more than enough."

DEAR INNER CHILD,

I KNOW YOU'VE BEEN HURT.
I WANT YOU TO KNOW THAT
YOU ARE LOVED, THERE IS
NOTHING WRONG WITH YOU,
+ YOU'RE ENOUGH,
JUST AS YOU ARE.
YOU ARE SAFE,
I PROMISE.

Take 5: Nurture Your Inner Child

Ask yourself in random moments, such as when you're looking in the mirror in the morning, boiling the kettle, or traveling to work:

* What does my inner child most need to hear?

And then offer yourself kind words that correspond to this, whether out loud or in your own head. Your innate ability to offer love is the key to your healing and personal growth.

CULTIVATING SAFETY

Ensuring safety for ourselves—both in our relationships with others and in our relationship with ourselves—is an important part of learning to reparent ourselves, and therefore starting to heal from emotional wounds that were formed during our childhood.

A question I come back to time and again, within both my personal reparenting journey and in my therapeutic work with clients is: "Did we feel safe when we were young?"

The common response to this in the absence of physical abuse is: "Yes. Of course, I was safe." And this may be true on a physical level. But what about on an emotional level?

When we feel emotionally safe, we feel able to fully express our authentic selves and share even the most vulnerable parts of ourselves.

How emotionally safe we felt as children depends on how safe it felt to:

* Show our emotions
* Express our opinions
* Share our goals and dreams
* Be honest about our fears
* Not have *all* the answers
* Make mistakes
* Seek affection
* Cry and feel sad
* Ask for help
* Ask questions
* Play and pretend
* Say no.

Take 5: Establish Your Sense of Emotional Safety

Take a moment to consider how emotionally safe you felt as a child by asking yourself the following questions:

* Could I voice an opinion without fear of physical or verbal reprimands? Could I speak about a delicate topic without fearing humiliation?
* What happened when I cried?
* What happened when I felt excited, or sad?
* What happened when I asked for help or said no?

When a child feels unsafe, either emotionally or physically, they may subconsciously look for a modicum, or an illusion, of safety by playing one of the following roles in life:

* The High Achiever
* The Family Therapist
* The "Good" Child
* The Parent
* The Joker
* The Rebel

If you recognize any of these as a role that you have adopted within your family structure, and maybe even that you still adopt in whatever your everyday situation is now, bring these findings back to the first pillar, Inner-Child Healing, and begin to unpack the purpose of this role further.

Cultivating Safety in Our Relationships

We all have many types of relationships in our lives: familial, friendships, co-workers, romantic…Whatever the dynamic, these interactions can feel either emotionally healthy and "safe," or emotionally unhealthy and "unsafe."

One of our roles, as a newly conscious inner parent, is to be discerning about who our inner child spends their time with. After all, any good parent wants to make sure that their child spends their time with people who are kind to them and who make them feel good about themselves, i.e. who are emotionally safe!

Qualities of emotionally safe people include being:

* Accepting
* Supportive
* Respectful
* Self-aware
* Clear with boundaries
* Consistent
* A good communicator

* A good listener
* Accountable for their own actions

Qualities of emotionally unsafe people include being:

* Volatile
* Unreflective
* Intrusive or controlling
* Hostile to emotional expression
* Defensive
* Dismissive
* Inconsistent and unclear
* Unpredictable

It's important to bear in mind that nobody is all one thing or another—in this case neither 100 percent emotionally safe nor 100 percent emotionally unsafe. Not even us. We all exhibit behaviors from time to time that fall into the unsafe category.

That being said, it would be a good idea to pause and take a deeper look at the health and function of any relationship in which unsafe characteristics become a recurring or ongoing pattern, rather than a rarity.

Our level of safety can often be determined simply by the "vibe" we get from another person—the inner spidey-sense that sometimes tells us: "This is not a person I feel comfortable being vulnerable with." Or "This is not a person that I should trust."

Take 5: Explore How People Make You Feel

The greatest doorway we have to our own truth is our body. So after you spend time in a particular person's company, take a few moments to reflect on the effect it has had on you. Ask yourself:

* How do I feel in my body around this person?
* Do I leave their company feeling (generally) confident and content, or defeated and "down"?
* What generally makes me feel safe in relationships?
* And what would make me feel safer in this relationship?

It's important to acknowledge that we cannot create a sense of safety in any relationship that is actively abusive. Some would say that this also applies to relationships that were historically abusive, even if they are no longer so.

Feeling safe takes time and practice. On the pages that follow is a range of ways to help build your sense of emotional safety within non-abusive relationships:

Instead of Interrupting, Hold Your Thoughts

We develop emotional safety in our relationships when we make the effort to actively listen to one another. This happens when you place your concentration solely on the other person that you are with—no mobile phone, no laptop, no TV; when you make eye contact; when you are mindful of your facial expressions; when you encourage the other person—whether partner, friend, family member, or whatever else—to share; and when you, all the while, hold on to your own thoughts until the other person is finished speaking.

Instead of Judgment, Lead with Curiosity

It can be really difficult not to judge what another person is saying if we dislike or disagree with what we're hearing. But the hard truth is that just because someone is saying something we don't like, it doesn't make them wrong or a bad person. They're probably expressing something that feels true for them. And we'll never build our emotional safety if all we ever do is criticize.

So, outside of abusive situations where people might be trying to manipulate or control you, rather than shutting someone down with judgment and criticism, try to respond with curiosity instead.

You can do this by asking questions to try to better understand where they're coming from before you decide how you might like to respond. Try to remember when having such interactions just how much you care for the other person and how much they mean to you—to make it easier for you to stem your judgments.

Instead of Reacting, Practice Pausing

Part of emotional safety is knowing that we can share without fear of being either humiliated or harmed, even if we are sharing painful truths. As such, it is your responsibility to practice self-regulation when a loved one shares something with you, even if this turns out to be a difficult thing to hear.

Part of this is being able to pause rather than immediately flying off the handle in the heat of the moment. Just one second is all you need to start with. If you can create one second before responding, you can create two. From two, you can create three, and so on. Our reactions in situations like this show the other person what we believe is OK, so has the power to either give them the space to be themselves or to shut them down and make them feel bad.

Instead of Defending, Seek to Validate

Research carried out by the prestigious research center The Gottman Institute, found that two thirds of couples' arguments have no resolution. So, the next time you're in an argument, rather than attempting to get your partner (or friend) onto the same page as you by defending your own opinions, why not try to understand their side without trying to change their mind (even if we don't agree with what they're saying).

If both parties are willing to validate the other's opinion in this way, rather than jumping into detail about the many ways in which we perceive them to be wrong or misguided, it can work wonders for the sense of emotional safety within the relationship.

So instead of responding with something like "I don't know why you'd think that," try a validating statement, such as "It doesn't feel good to hear this / I'm not sure that I agree with you—but I understand what you're saying."

Instead of Internalizing, Lean into Communication

Emotional safety is something that it's worth having open conversations about with the people close to you. If you need an icebreaker, you might even consider chatting about this portion of the book with them to get things going.

For example, it can be immensely useful to let your loved ones know which behaviors make you feel safe and which don't. Another important conversation in terms of emotional safety can be about boundaries, as covered in Chapter 6. An open chat about this might allow us to communicate, for example, that we no longer feel comfortable, or "safe," talking about a certain person or topic in a certain way.

More often than not, internalization brews resentment. Emotional safety (and trust) therefore requires us to be vulnerable by being brave enough to communicate openly about our experiences and our needs.

Cultivating Safety in Ourselves

Having hopefully now established just how important creating and promoting emotional safety within our relationships is to the process of reparenting, it's also now crucial to understand the need to create emotional safety within ourselves. So here follows a range of ways in which you can start to do this:

Identify Anchors

If you have a good sense of what makes you feel safe and unsafe in different aspects of your life, you can use these things as anchors that strengthen your sense of safety any time you need them. So:

1. Get a piece of paper and a pen.
2. Then take a few moments to identify ways that contribute to your sense of safety using the questions below:

What makes me feel safe in my body?

What makes me feel safe in a relationship?

What makes me feel safe financially?

What makes me feel grounded?

When do I feel unsafe? What does that feel like, physically?

What can I do to create emotional safety when I'm feeling unsafe?

What would enhance my sense of safety in my life?

Fortunately, many of the things that can often help us feel a sense of safety are easily accessible. For example, a conversation with a loved one, gulping in some much-needed fresh air, or time spent with a pet. Some others may prove a little more challenging to find at any given time—either because they are "relational" anchors that require other people (such as a friend, a parent, or a therapist) or "planned" anchors that require more of an element of advance planning, patience, and dedicated time.

Examples of accessible safety anchors include:

* Breath work
* Time with a pet
* A walk in nature
* Setting a boundary on a social engagement

Examples of relational anchors include:

* A conversation with a loved one
* A cinema trip or other outing with a friend
* A session with a therapist

Examples of planned anchors include:

* Changing a pattern of behavior
* Saving money
* Moving out of a toxic environment

Keep your Contracts

Another important part of reparenting involves learning to trust yourself. A simple way you can begin to do this is to make small regular commitments to yourself that you stick to.

It might not feel like a big deal when you say "I'm going to do X, Y, or Z tomorrow" and you then choose not to do it for some reason. But, over time, this making and breaking of tiny self-promises has a big impact, as the small commitments that you don't keep create a deficit in the trust you have in yourself and in your sense of feeling heard and valued.

By keeping small, regular contracts you can build your level of self-trust, strengthen your confidence and self-esteem, and show your inner child that your word really matters.

If you find that you're continually breaking small self-contracts, it may be a sign that they need some scaling back or that they might not be the right ones for you right now, so you may be best to reassess them.

Identify Unsafe Inner Behaviors

We all display "unsafe" emotional behavior from time to time. So part of establishing a sense of strong emotional safety within yourself lies in identifying any unsafe behaviors that you yourself may exhibit. Identifying which of these behaviors are sporadic and which are more habitual can provide useful insight into what your deep-set issues are.

When you recognize an unsafe behavior, such as putting off a doctor's appointment, turning to substances in times of stress, or texting an ex when you feel lonely, it is useful to ask yourself:

What might this behavior be masking?

What need do I have that is not being met?

How can I address this need?

How can I soothe myself in this moment of feeling unsafe?

Do I feel I want to communicate how I feel with another person?

If so, how can I do that in a way that they'll hear me?

How do I want to feel when I leave this conversation? What would that entail?

It's important not to let the recognition of unsafe behaviors become in any way an opportunity to shame yourself; this wouldn't lead anywhere good. Recognition of such behaviors is simply a sign of growing self-awareness in your journey of self-discovery, so provides an opportunity to hold yourself gently, hold yourself accountable, and realign your behavior in a way that feels more authentic and helpful to you moving forward.

REPARENTING AS A FORM OF SELF-CARE

At its center, reparenting is a practice of self-care, as it requires learning how to take care of our own needs, both as the child we once were and the adult we are today. Self-care involves becoming more aware of the patterns and beliefs that drive our thoughts and behaviors, and making decisions every day that are in our own best interests as well as in the best interest of our relationships with those around us. Gradually, this process of reparenting will feel like coming home.

We each know ourselves better than anyone (even our therapist if we have one!). So, much as a loving and attentive parent can decipher the needs of their children, you already consciously or unconsciously know a great deal about your inner child and what they might need. Checking in and honoring your needs regularly will fine-tune this knowledge and reassure your inner child that you can take care of them.

So, for example, when you notice you're hungry, consider how you would parent a child who was feeling similar. Would you tell them to suck it up and hold tight for two hours, or would you go and source a snack to satisfy the hunger cue until dinner's ready? If you feel exhausted or overwhelmed, consider how you would parent a child feeling the same? Would you tell them "Too bad" and force them to push on? Or would you listen to them and offer comfort? What about when a child makes

EXAMPLES OF SMALL DAILY COMMITMENTS:

- GETTING UP AT 8AM
- MEDITATING FOR 5 MINUTES IN THE MORNING
- GOING FOR A QUICK STROLL AFTER BREAKFAST
- READING TEN PAGES OF YOUR CURRENT BOOK
- 10 MINUTES JOURNALING BEFORE BED
- BEING IN BED BY 10PM

a mistake? Would you scold them and constantly remind them of it or would you empathize and remind them that mistakes are a part of life, congratulate them for being courageous, and ask them what they've learned?

Take 5: Create a Routine

As part of your self-care reparenting routine, it's good to get into the habit of:

* Asking yourself regularly: "What do I need in this moment?"
* Practice honoring this need, without guilt.

As a parent to yourself, remember that just because you could physically do something, doesn't necessarily mean that you will have the capacity to do it in any moment. So always take time to assess how you're feeling and what you have the space and energy for in the present moment.

Scenarios will sometimes come up in which you have to push on through regardless of how you feel, but circumstances that won't benefit from a comforting chat with your inner parent are, ultimately, likely to be few and far between. And as you begin to honor your inner child, so you'll find that you're increasingly honoring your whole self.

THE ART OF SELF-DISCIPLINE

Another piece of the reparenting jigsaw is the art of self-discipline. We aren't born with the ability to manage our impulses and to discipline ourselves; it's something we learn in childhood—through the family home, the school system, extracurricular activities, and so on. And if we don't learn in a balanced, fair way in childhood, our relationship with self-discipline can often be quite skewed in adulthood.

If our early caregiver was, for example, scattered, absent, or yielded easily, our impulses may dictate our choices as adults and we may often opt for instant gratification over gentle discipline and delayed gratification. If, on the other hand, a caregiver was particularly domineering or cruel, we may fall the other way, with self-discipline becoming a practice of self-punishment. We all respond differently to compromised lessons in childhood.

If, on the other hand, our main caregivers had rules that they firmly and lovingly asserted and followed up on, they will have given us a good model for self-discipline in later life. Examples of this might have been cleaning your room before you were allowed out to play, practicing the piano before watching TV, or doing your homework before spending the evening on MSN messenger.

IF WE GREW
UP IN A CHAOTIC
ENVIRONMENT,
WE MAY MISTAKE
INTENSITY FOR
INTIMACY + SAFETY
FOR DANGER

Take 5: Assess Your Experience of Discipline

To ascertain what your current relationship with self-discipline is likely to be, ask yourself the following questions:

* What did discipline look like for me in childhood?
* How did my main caregiver assert rules? Firmly and lovingly? Scattered? Nonexistent? Domineeringly? Or other?
* Did this give me a good model for self-discipline?

As kids, the last thing we wanted to do was fill the dishwasher, vacuum the sitting room, or spend hours poring over a subject in school that had us at our wit's end (business studies for me!). But the reparenting process requires us to realign our view of discipline—to start seeing it as a way to focus our energy, build our patience, and feel more satisfied in, and prouder of, our choices.

The practice of self-discipline is key to showing our inner child that they are being looked after. If you were left alone or with a babysitter at a young age, you might have reveled in a few parent-free hours, but eventually you may have wondered what time your caregiver would return. The same can be said for the inner child. Self-discipline shows that, although there may be some time to run amuck parent-free, the parent will, in the end, return to keep them safe.

Please know that if you struggle with self-discipline, it doesn't mean you're weak-willed. By considering what self-discipline looked like for you growing up, realigning its meaning and starting to keep small daily contracts with yourself (as suggested on page 253), you will begin to separate the idea of discipline from how you may have viewed it when you were young (e.g. as self-punishment!). And you will therefore be able to integrate it more easily into your life.

REPARENTING AS A MEANS OF SELF-NOURISHMENT

Authentically nourishing yourself is much simpler than the media would sometimes make it appear, with its ever-changing obsessions with things like elaborate superfoods, expensive products, and obscure rituals. In fact, the process of reparenting could in itself be viewed as a form of pretty well-rounded self-nourishment.

Take 5: Identify the Nourishment Required

Below are some questions to help guide you toward what type of nourishment you may need to fill up on at any particular time:

* How well do I feel in my body?
* How well do I feel in my mind?
* How well do I feel in my environment?
* Am I connecting to others?
* Am I connecting with nature?

* Am I moving my body in a way that is enjoyable for me?
* Am I sleeping enough?
* Am I practicing self-regulation?
* Am I drinking enough water?
* Am I enjoying my food?
* Am I depriving myself in any way?
* Am I feeling supported with my mental health?
* Do I need any additional support?

Looking at your answers, are there some areas you could bring more conscious attention to? Perhaps you could do with more sleep? Or additional mental health support?

It's really important not to allow self-care and self-nourishment to become "shoulds" that you berate yourself with. Instead, use your answers above as a gentle guide for ways that you can begin to be mindful of introducing more consistent self-nourishment and self-parenting into your day-to-day life.

Although we can continue on our journey of self-discovery and self-enhancement without a therapist, psychologist, or psychiatrist, it is not always safe to do so, particularly if we've experienced severe trauma.

So remember that self-care, self-nourishment, and self-parenting (or reparenting) are *for* the self, not *by* the self. So, although time alone can serve us well, if we ever start feeling disconnected from people, overwhelmed by the path we're on, lacking in support, or feeling that our attempts at self-care and reparenting are turning into emotional isolation and re-traumatization, then be sure to reach out for help.

We're all social creatures (you too, fellow introverts!), and healing is relational. So even when it can feel hard, connecting with another human and accepting their help and support can be one of the greatest ways that we care for ourselves, and subsequently, others.

MENTAL NOTES

Take five minutes at the end of each day for a month to reflect on the following:

* What way can I connect with my inner child? And what does my inner child need to hear? (E.g. you are smart, you are loved …)
* How might I strengthen my sense of safety in life? (E.g. I can practice breathwork more often and make more time for my friend …)
* What is one small daily contract I can make with myself? (E.g. I will go for a very short walk every morning. I will put my phone down by 10 p.m. …)
* What adjectives would I use to describe my inner parent today? And how would I like my inner parent to be moving forward? (E.g. empowering, understanding, critical, wary, nurturing …)

By the end of the month, you'll have created a treasure chest of information about how you can start to heal your inner child through the process of reparenting, including ideas of how you would like to treat yourself moving forward so that you feel as safe and loved as we all deserve to.

8.
Going
Beyond
the Self

HOW TO BE A
GOOD FRIEND

"Shame dies when stories are told in safe places."
Ann Voskamp

We all go through challenging times, and there's no doubt that authentic connection with others can help us through such times. This means not only us being able to reach out to others for help and support, but also others being able to reach out to us. So how can we go beyond our own issues and concerns—to be a good friend for those we love and care about?

FRIENDS IN NEED OF HELP

Most of us will, at some point, have had a loved one who has been struggling in some way with their mental health, so will recognize how difficult it can be to know how to support them. Most likely, you've wanted to do your very best by them, but you worry about saying something "wrong."

As a psychotherapist, I frequently see partners, friends, siblings, and other family members reach out looking for guidance on how to support their loved ones through mental hardships such as anxiety, depression, and trauma.

Even when it seems obvious that someone is going through a difficult time, there is often no simple way of knowing exactly what they're struggling with, especially if the person isn't yet able to understand or communicate what they are going through themselves; they may well not feel able to provide clear answers about what you can do to support them.

The good news, however, is that we usually don't need to know every detail in order to support them. It's generally more important that we just respond to someone in pain with sensitivity and care.

Whether the person in need is a partner, friend, family member, or someone we work with, there are many ways that we can support them.

My hope is that the insights in this chapter will help you understand more about what healthy help and support look like. But if you feel you need further help, then do, of course, reach out to a mental health professional for further guidance.

RECOGNIZING HEALTHY (VERSUS UNHEALTHY) SUPPORT

An integral part of any relationship is the willingness and ability to support one another, even through hard times. It's so important to know that we can trust and rely on one other.

There's nothing wrong with needing others; we've always lived in communities and relied on each other for survival. Healthy support involves mutual give and take—where all people in the relationship give and receive support, encouragement, and practical help in more or less equal measure. However, healthy relationships also acknowledge that there will be times when imbalance is inevitable. This is especially true when one of the people is in pain, struggling, or experiencing hardship.

The crucial thing here is that we ensure that such imbalance is only ever temporary. Otherwise, there can come a point when the support we offer becomes less healthy, potentially even entering into territory known in the world of therapy as "co-dependency."

Co-dependency describes any relationship in which one person's identity, self-worth, and self-esteem come from the presence and approval of another person. It is typically a trauma response to emotional neglect in early childhood or living in a household where there was some form of addiction.

Co-dependency occurs when we inadvertently start to define our role in a relationship through how much help we give to the other. In co-dependency, the care we give to the other is what gives our life meaning and purpose. Without it, we're unsure of who we are. "If you're happy, I'm happy" is the battle cry of co-dependency.

People who are in a pattern of co-dependency:

* Need to feel needed
* Can begin to feel empty without someone to care for
* Feel responsible for the other person's emotional state
* Can find it difficult being away from the other person
* Can find it difficult to form boundaries between themselves and the other person.

In healthy relationships, on the other hand, our identity and sense of purpose aren't enmeshed with needing to support or assist others; we simply do so because we wish to.

When giving healthy support, we:

* Enjoy offering our help but also know we're each capable of surviving by ourselves
* Respect the other person's autonomy
* Have a good sense of what is and isn't our responsibility
* Are willing to make some sacrifices to help the other, but also set limits to what we will do
* Value our own needs and desires too much to compromise or ignore them
* Don't seek to change another's behavior simply because it's not the way we'd do things.

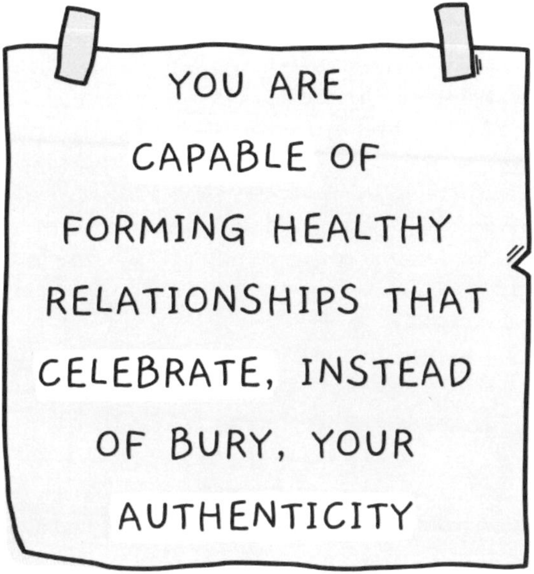
YOU ARE
CAPABLE OF
FORMING HEALTHY
RELATIONSHIPS THAT
CELEBRATE, INSTEAD
OF BURY, YOUR
AUTHENTICITY

Offering healthy support is great but if you find yourself being the "therapist" or wise monk to others with little or no reciprocity, or you find that you're consistently overextending yourself to be there for someone to the detriment of your own needs, you can start addressing this by establishing firmer boundaries (see Chapter 6), communicating your concerns to someone you trust, and/or seeking out a co-dependency support group.

Recognizing the difference between healthy support and co-dependency can be difficult, especially if we have never experienced a healthy interdependent relationship before. Taking the time to read more on co-dependency and healthy relationships—both in this book and beyond—is a great way to begin your journey beyond this pattern. But if you feel that you need more support than this in order to break old patterns and form more positive relationships in your life, then please do consider seeking professional help.

Take 5: Take Time to Reflect

If you identify with the patterns of co-dependency described on the previous pages, or identify as a recovering co-dependent, ask yourself:

In what ways could I provide support to those I love, yet not so much that I disappear into their emotional world?

Other questions to ponder when we recognize or suspect a co-dependent moment are:

* Am I holding space or giving advice?
* Am I sacrificing myself, my own wants, or my own boundaries?
* Am I being honest or self-censoring?
* Do I really have the time or energy for this?
* Have I identified and expressed my own needs here?
* What may have been triggering my old pattern?
* What can I remind myself of in this moment?

HOW TO OFFER HEALTHY SUPPORT

Once we know for sure that we're in a healthy, interdependent relationship with our loved ones, there are many ways in which we can be a good friend and help them.

Some of the best ways in which to support others are:

* Educating yourself
* Holding space
* Speaking but respecting
* Assisting, not insisting
* Minding your own mind

We will therefore explore each of these things in the pages below. Please note, however, that the guidance that follows is specifically for relationships that are neither co-dependent nor contain abuse of any kind.

If you find yourself looking to support a partner, friend, family member, or anyone else who is abusive in some way, please seek professional help. No amount of pain justifies manipulation, aggression, or violence.

Educating Yourself

Uncertainty can create a lot of stress. Taking the time to educate ourselves about the mental health struggles that a loved one is experiencing—whether trauma, anxiety, depression, or any other mental health condition— can help to alleviate some of this uncertainty and will also allow us to offer them more informed, and therefore hopefully more useful, support.

For example, if you are supporting someone with depression, it can be useful to know certain phrases to avoid when talking to them about their condition. Likewise, there are tropes that have weathered badly when it comes to anxiety and bipolar disorder that it's also best to steer clear of. Look up the facts through reputable resources, or seek out the support of a mental health professional.

Below you'll find some information on trauma that you can use as a starting point for your self-education. As a mental health practitioner, another's experience of trauma is something I meet nearly every day. "Trauma" is also a word that can create some confusion, and a term we often associate with war veterans. It extends well beyond that, and below you'll find some information that will guide your understanding of trauma further. Although this guidance is specific to trauma, much of it can also be applied to supporting people struggling in other ways.

You might even want to consider showing this section to your friend or loved one and asking for their feedback on what applies to them and what doesn't. Plus do feel free to take the time to read further afield if you would like to widen and deepen your understanding.

Understanding Trauma

Trauma is an inner response to an event or experience that overwhelms our capacity to process and cope. It impacts how we think, feel, perceive, and process—affecting us physically, socially, emotionally, and psychologically.

When we hear the word trauma, our thoughts might automatically go to something physical or associate the term with, as mentioned above, war veterans. However, *any* distressing event that negatively impacts our ability to process and cope can be considered trauma.

In traditional therapeutic terms, trauma is split into "big T" and "little t"—a distinction that can create some confusion at best and stigma at worst. To clarify—this distinction is not a reflection on the severity of the trauma, but a distinction on the process and duration of each type.

"Big T" events tend to be singular experiences that leave a person feeling hopeless or powerless, such as a natural disaster, sexual assault, terrorist attack, or car accident.

"Little t" events are not necessarily visible yet are chronically distressing, with a serious and debilitating effect on our ability to cope. Examples of "little t" may be a divorce, childhood emotional neglect, exposure to bullying, financial difficulty, or ongoing emotional abuse.

Stress and trauma exist on a continuum. Excess stress takes a huge toll which can develop into complex trauma.

"Big T" isn't "worse" or "more serious" than "little t." Although these are the clinical names of the categories, there is no such thing as a small trauma. Trauma is a fundamental feeling of threat and a perceived lack of safety. It is different for everyone and, although the division may be clinically useful for practitioners, as the experiencer, the severity of our trauma cannot be defined by category names.

Physical symptoms of trauma include but are not limited to fatigue, difficulty concentrating, a more sensitive startle response (which causes us to flinch or jump more regularly), changes to the menstrual cycle, and the potential onset of autoimmune illnesses such as rheumatoid arthritis, inflammatory bowel disease, as well as insomnia, depression, and anxiety.

Socially, trauma may make it hard to trust others' intentions. We can feel disconnected from day-to-day life and find we snap at others more frequently. We might begin to isolate and avoid meeting friends. And/or we can become overwhelmed in public spaces, as well as feeling hypercritical of ourselves and others.

The emotional impact of trauma can result in a preoccupation and worry over minor details. We can feel the need to make big, impulsive changes. We may experience a sense of hollowness, with our days feeling empty and flat. And/or we might feel we disappoint others in our life and struggle with excessive doubt.

Psychologically, trauma impacts the brain function in many complex ways. Three of the most researched changes occur in the amygdala (fear center), the prefrontal cortex (thinking center), and the anterior cingulate cortex (emotion regulation center). A traumatized brain's thinking and emotional regulation centers may become under-activated, with the fear center becoming over-activated. This is why traumatized people can find it difficult to concentrate, engage, and soothe themselves, while simultaneously feeling out of control, irritated, or on edge, anticipating danger.

As a result, psychological symptoms of trauma can include: flashbacks, insomnia, nightmares, loss of time, dissociation, derealization (an alteration on the experience of our reality so that things seem unreal), feeling disconnected, increased hypervigilance, and difficulty recalling memories.

What is upsetting or wounding for one person can be traumatic for another, and vice versa. And while we all have wounds, we are not all traumatized.

Understanding the effects of a trauma on someone is more significant to determining trauma than the event itself. There is no definition or person that can override the experience, memory, magnitude of the experience, and the sense that something was traumatic. Trauma is trauma and whatever the experience, it deserves our respect, compassion, and empathy.

Holding Space

Perhaps you've heard this term "holding space" before. Maybe from a friend beginning therapy for the first time, or as you've been scrolling through social media. But what does it really mean?

Put simply, holding space means truly allowing "space" for another person, or making the moment about that other person. Whether you're talking on the phone or chatting over coffee, you are present and listening, without judgment.

Holding space is more than biting your tongue and not interrupting. It means putting your opinions to the side and allowing someone the wide-open space to speak about what is happening for them. Sometimes this may require just listening. Sometimes a little dialogue. Other times, it may mean just sitting with them in silence.

Holding space involves us surrendering our need for control and, rather than imposing our own history, knowledge, or structure on another's experience, following the other person with *their* thoughts and what *they* need in that moment.

It sounds like a lot, and it is. Holding space can be difficult to do, but it's not a complex concept in itself and is possibly even something that you already engage in. For example, if you're a person that people tend to pour their hearts out to in supermarket queues, it is likely that you already know how to listen without criticizing or trying to fix every problem.

Holding space can be as ordinary as that. However, most of us tend to struggle with being able to "hold space" in this way with those in our inner circle. This is mainly because we are so close to them. It's really difficult to maintain healthy distance, objectivity, and emotional space. We come to these relationships with prior knowledge and presumptions—factors that can make holding space a little trickier.

HOLDING SPACE FOR
ANOTHER PERSON MEANS THAT:

-WE LISTEN AND OBSERVE
WITHOUT JUDGMENT
-WE DON'T DISMISS OR INSIST.
WE ARE OPEN TO WHATEVER
COMES
-WE DON'T RACE IN WITH
SOLUTIONS OR OUR OWN
EXPERIENCES
-WE DON'T TRY TO RESCUE,
FIX THE PROBLEM, OR OFFER
ANOTHER PERSPECTIVE
-WE ARE PRESENT AND
ACCEPTING, PARKING ANY
SHOULDS

Take 5:

Let's take a moment to consider how much space we feel others hold for us in our everyday lives. How often do you feel that you can speak openly and safely about something personal without fearing judgment, however subtle?

If you're in therapy or have a friend or partner adept at holding space, then the likelihood is regularly. But unfortunately, this isn't the case for many people, and it isn't until we experience the value of this space that we truly realize what's been missing. In its presence, we realize its absence.

We're not typically taught to hold space. And for most people—particularly those who grew up with siblings—pockets of uninterrupted space dedicated just to them have been fleeting in life, or a valuable commodity grasped only very occasionally. Holding space is a valuable skill to be learned.

As we become more adept at being fully present and parking our opinions on the sidelines, we will begin to get more of a feel for when gentle guidance seems most apt versus when withholding our own thoughts seems like the wiser option. For example, we may want to give our two cents if the person asks for it or feels too lost to know what to ask for. On the other hand, we would do better to hold back if our guidance, however gentle, might contribute to a person feeling inadequate or foolish.

It's always worth checking in with ourselves whether we are offering solutions to help alleviate the pain in others or, underneath it, whether we are looking to alleviate a discomfort that has appeared in ourselves? Someone else's struggles can bring up all sorts of uncomfortable thoughts and emotions in ourselves so we should take time to pay attention to these.

There is a careful dance that we all must learn to do when we hold space for others. Spotting the areas in which the person feels most vulnerable and learning whether to offer or withhold takes practice, missteps, and a bit of humility. But it's worth keeping practicing this dance, as it can help others more than we often realize.

Speaking But Respecting

Mental health stigma, both explicit and implicit, is unfortunately alive and well. Implicit stigma may show up as a reluctance to acknowledge the pain of another out of our own discomfort or a fear of embarrassing them. Although our heart may be in the right place, avoidance of mental health conversations serves only to increase the stigma and therefore the shame surrounding it.

If a friend went to the doctor with a stomach bug, we'd check in with them to see how it went. Yet, on the whole, we're not as quick to ask how a therapy session or an appointment with a psychiatrist went. So check in with your loved ones. Send a message. Ask them about it when it's just the two of you. It may feel awkward at first but that's OK. Most progressive conversations start off this way. Allow the person you care about to speak about what's on their mind even if they become upset. And try your best to stay grounded, calm, and just listen.

If your loved one is not open to speaking about their experiences, there's no need to demand it or plow on, regardless of their wishes. Respect their boundaries. They may need time to be alone and reflect on their thoughts. As a rule of thumb, it's good to offer your support and then offer it again. This way, you make it clear that your help is there if needed, without insisting they take it.

This might sound like:

"You seem down today. Would you like to talk about it?"

If they say no, consider adding in: "Are you sure? I'm here if you need me" or "Please know that you can call me any time you might feel in need of a friendly ear or a chat."

If they still say no, let it be.

In offering your help twice, you make a strong bid for connection—and give a clear sign that you're open and willing to listen, as well as that you care and are there should they need someone.

If your loved one then *does* choose to speak about what is happening for them, just be mindful not to assume that this means they're looking for you to give advice or to "fix" things for them.

If someone you know is struggling or you suspect they're in pain, it can be hard to start a conversation with them about what's going on. If a face-to-face chat feels too intimidating, consider sending a text or an email. There is no "perfect" time to start a conversation on mental health, but ideally try setting aside an hour or more, so that you don't feel under time pressure or have to cut the conversation short.

See the "Take 5" below for some prompts to help you with what you might say in terms of what has caused you to feel concerned.

Don't worry if you feel uncomfortable. Feeling uncomfortable is part of the process. It won't last. Tomorrow is often the day we save for our best intentions. Instead, start a conversation today.

Take 5: Start a Conversation

Sometimes, we want to help but we simply don't have the words. Here you'll find some prompts to guide you when you're looking to start a conversation regarding a loved one's mental health. Read through the examples and personalize them as you go.

* I've noticed over the last [length of time] that you seem to have been feeling angry/sad/distracted/stressed …
* Lately, I've noticed that you've lost interest in [thing you enjoy]/not been sleeping/been skipping meals/been drinking more often …
* Bringing it up makes me feel embarrassed/silly/anxious/nervous but …
* I'm mentioning this because I'm worried about you/I'm afraid/I want you to know I care/I don't know what to do or say/I don't know if you've talked to someone else about how you're feeling/it's affecting our relationship …
* I would like to help you feel supported/talk about this more/talk to a doctor/talk to a therapist/find a support group/figure out a plan. What could I do that will help?

If your loved one is willing to engage in conversation, it's worth noting, as mentioned earlier within the section on trauma, that there are certain phrases we may fall into saying out of frustration or misplaced love that can have a negative impact on the person we're trying to offer love and care to, however well intentioned we might be.

So try and avoid statements like:

* "Things aren't so bad."
* "It's your own fault."
* "Things could be much worse."
* "You wouldn't be experiencing this if God thought you couldn't handle it."
* "[Person's Name] has it worse than you do."
* "You don't look anxious/depressed."
* "Life isn't fair, is it?"
* "There's nothing wrong with you."
* "It's just in your head."
* "You need to get out more."
* "Snap out of it/Get over it/Move on."
* "Just be positive/happy!"
* "Good vibes only."
* "Have you tried [latest pseudo-health trend here]?"
* "Well…Shakespeare wrote *King Lear* in a pandemic."

Instead, lead with validation and kindness, which sounds more like:

* "It's OK to feel this way."
* "It's probably really hard to see any good in this situation right now."
* "There doesn't always have to be a silver lining."
* "You are important to me."

* "I love you."
* "You're not crazy, and you're not alone. I'm here."
* "I might not understand it, but I want to."
* "I'm sorry that you're in so much pain."
* "I can take care of myself, so you don't need to worry that your pain is burdening me."
* "You are not a burden."

Assisting, Not Insisting

Supporting someone effectively means appreciating each person's differences and recognizing that these differences can lead to them making choices that *we* wouldn't necessarily make. Although we want to help and we might do things and manage situations differently, it's always worth considering, before offering any words of "wisdom" whether you're "assisting" or "insisting."

Our way isn't necessarily the right way. As such, it's important to allow your loved ones to make their own decisions and to have different experiences from us.

When someone we care for is struggling or in pain, it's all too easy to try to tell them our answers in an attempt to save and rescue them. Although this might make us feel lighter, it can lead to the other person feeling isolated ("My problem is burdening them. It's probably better if I don't mention it again"); feeling inadequate ("They don't think I'm able to manage this by myself"); and/or experiencing more emotional pain. When we aren't in a great place, time and again what we need, more often than not, is someone who will simply *listen*. We don't want someone who is "insisting" on "fixing" us; we just want to know that you care. This is what will "assist" us.

Offering care with a listening and curious ear goes a much longer way than offering possible solutions or ways to "snap out" of what the other person is experiencing.

Offering care, or "assisting" someone, can be as straightforward as repeating what your friend said back to them—to help them get clarity. It can be as ordinary as asking questions, without attempting to sway them from their own decisions. It can be an invite to the cinema, a walk, or a coffee, even when we're fairly sure the offer will be turned down. So just see what feels right in the moment.

If it ever feels as though advice might be necessary, check with the person first to see if they're open to hearing it. If they are, offer it gently, without hope or agenda. Be patient. We don't need to know the full story in order to offer our support. Just being there can be helpful for someone who may want to open up at a later point.

Naturally, there are situations where we intuitively know that it is in the best interest of our loved one (and maybe also others) that we speak up, especially when it concerns the physical and emotional safety of others. Listen to your gut about this and exercise discernment.

If you are worried that someone is in danger, experiencing abuse, or may take their own life, speak to someone you trust, your local doctor, or a mental health professional as soon as possible. Specialist mental health organizations such as the Samaritans offer invaluable 24/7 services.

Sometimes our support as friends just won't be enough. So if someone close to you continues to struggle after weeks or months, don't be afraid to encourage them to seek direct help from a mental health professional. You could offer to help them find a provider, if needed. And, if there are difficult decisions to be made, you could offer to talk through the options with them.

Minding Your Own Mind

Some of us can be adept at taking care of others to the detriment of our own wellbeing. If you fall into this category, you might feel that speaking to someone else about supporting a loved one would be a betrayal of their trust or self-indulgent. But "minding your own mind" is anything but this! It is so important for you to speak to someone about your own feelings as you support others with theirs—to ensure that you stay well within yourself.

Take psychotherapists for example. Most therapists will be in therapy themselves, as well having the support of things like personal supervision sessions, group supervision sessions, and workshops with their peers. As clinicians, we have to keep our tanks full in order to be able to continue to sit with, and hold space for, so many clients experiencing hardship.

Therapists aside, anyone who is trying to offer support to others and who isn't in the greatest headspace risks breaking down and getting unwell themselves if they try to continue to provide all the care and attention that they wish they could offer.

It stands to reason that if we're feeling full to the brim with anxiety and stress ourselves, we're most likely not in the best position to hold space for another's anxiety and stress. We can't share a resource with others that we're lacking ourselves.

Through self-discovery, we learn how to become a healthy support for others and, while we're actively healing, we will inevitable slip up here and there. The healing process requires that we don't berate ourselves when we stumble but catch and care for ourselves after the fall.

Take 5: Give Yourself a Regular Check-Up

It's important to regularly check in with yourself and take stock of your own mental health. Ask yourself the following questions every now and then:

* How am I doing?
* Is there anything I need in this moment?
* How am I sleeping? How is my appetite?
* What do I need to do to stay more balanced and present?
* What do I have the emotional bandwidth for today?
* What changes might I need to make to the structure of my days in order to feel better in myself?

Helping others shouldn't hurt you, so be sure to take time for yourself, too:

* Find your own support system
* Draw your own boundaries
* Respect your own limits

* Take time to process your own feelings
* Journal, meditate, or do whatever else that brings you a sense of calm
* Spend time doing things you enjoy.

It's really important to recognize what we have the capacity for at any given point, and to do this without guilt or shame. Only by continually recognizing, prioritizing, and honoring our own needs—as part of our ongoing journey of self-discovery—can we put ourselves in the best place to offer our help and support to others in their times of need.

IT IS ONLY
BY RESPECTING
OUR LIMITS + OUR
RESPONSIBILITY AS A
FRIEND, THAT WE
PROVIDE THE MOST
EFFECTIVE SUPPORT IN
THE LONG RUN

MENTAL NOTES

Take five minutes at the end of each day for a month to reflect on the following:

* What examples of healthy and unhealthy support did I display and/or witness today? [E.g. I asked a friend if they'd like some input on an issue they're dealing with and respected their decision when they said no…]
* How have others held space for me today? How did that feel? [E.g. my partner rang me after work to hear about my day. I felt seen and I felt loved…]

* What can I take from my answers above to guide what my support looks like going forward? [E.g. the small things like a quick call matter. I can incorporate that more with friends going forward…]

* What do I need to mind my own mental health while supporting others? [E.g. it's important I make time to listen to the podcast I love. It's important I get out for a walk tomorrow…]

After the month, you'll have mounds of material on what healthy and unhealthy support looks like, how to hold space, and ways to support your mental health as you show up for others.

AFTERWORD

And so, we're at an end! Or perhaps it's a beginning? The beginning of your continuous journey of self-discovery, learning more about who you are and where you want to be.

Whether you have read this book from cover to cover or dipped in and out, I hope you found some snippets of insight.

Goodbyes have never been my strong point. In my haste for the moment to be over, I'm often left holding on to something that I wish I had shared—a sentiment, a gratitude, a reflection. This is a pattern that I don't want to repeat with you! So here are the last three considerations that I would like to share with you, which I'd kick myself later if I forgot to say.

I. GO EASY ON YOURSELF

I mean it. You deserve a sustainable journey. Don't burn out trying to discover and implement everything at once. Don't berate yourself if some parts of this book feel like too much for you right now. Just come back when you're ready. I, too, struggle, resist, deny, and avoid at times. I'm far from "my highest self." I don't have much interest in pursuing that ideal. But I'm on the path and learning along the way. So we're in the trenches together, discovering ways to better deal with things when the going gets tough—with love and compassion at the heart of everything we learn and do.

2. DON'T BE AFRAID TO ASK FOR HELP

There's an old Irish expression—*Giorraíonn beirt bóthar*—that means "Two people shorten the road"—and I really believe this. So please never feel you have to travel on your journey of self-development alone. Some years ago, I went looking for professional mental health support. My initial experience was neither positive nor pleasant but, to this day, I'm thankful that I didn't stop there. Instead, I kept searching and found an amazing therapist who I then stayed with for three years. It isn't an exaggeration to say that, without her, this book wouldn't exist. In fact, without her, there would be no "me" quite as I am today. One bad experience doesn't translate to "All mental health support is bad." So please keep looking for the help that you need—whether from loved ones, support groups, or accredited therapists (see the Further Resources list on page 296 as a starting point for this). And be sure to draw on your support network when you're running on empty.

3. SELF-DISCOVERY IS A LIFELONG PROCESS, BUT MORE THAN THAT, IT'S A LIFELONG OPPORTUNITY

You're not going to stop discovering, changing, or growing when you reach a certain age or a certain stage on your self-discovery journey—and nor should you have to! I want you to live *exploring*, I want you to live *feeling*. But, more than anything, I want you to live *curiously*. You deserve to live a life that embraces all the possibilities of imperfection. You deserve to live a life that doesn't sacrifice either breadth or depth. You deserve to enjoy the lifetime of opportunities that lies ahead of you.

This is your moment. If you allow it. If you embrace it.

You in?

FURTHER RESOURCES

To see more of my work, you'll find me over on Instagram @TheMindGeek. Come say hi!

The below resources will help you in furthering your knowledge on certain topics and in expanding your support systems.

MENTAL HEALTH SUPPORT WEBSITES

APA.org
BetterHelp.com
NAMI.org
PsychologyTools.com
TalkSpace.com

APPS

Calm
Headspace

BOOKS

Levine, Dr. Amir and Heller, Rachel, *Attached*, 2019, Bluebird

O' Morain, Padraig, *Daily Calm*, 2019, Yellow Kite

Perry, Philippa, *The Book You Wish Your Parents Had Read (and Your Children Will be Glad That You Did)*, 2019, Penguin Life

Stanley, Elizabeth A., *Widen the Window*, 2019, Yellow Kite

Van der Kolk, Bessel, *The Body Keeps the Score*, 2015, Penguin

OTHER

Having said all this, I've found the resources that often work best for me have been:

A therapist I trust
A good friend
A great book to escape into
A strong cup of tea
A hug from my partner
A journal or piece of paper to write in/on
So be mindful not to write off these kinds of fundamentals.

ACKNOWLEDGMENTS

This book is more than myself. It is pieced together by the distilled wisdom of all those who have held my heart and those I've walked beside. Without you all, these words wouldn't be here.

To my fiancée, Claire Kennelly, you not only supported me through the ugliest of tears, you physically constructed a writing corner in our small apartment so I could write by fairy light on the dreariest of days. Thank you for your unwavering belief when I had lost my own. I can think of no one else I could have traversed this pandemic-writing experience with. I love you so much.

Louise Eccles, I know I've quoted this to you time and again, but I'll do it once more for good measure. In her book *American Wife*, Curtis Sittenfeld wrote: "She was the reason I was a reader, and being a reader was what had made me most myself." I'll never forget you bestowing me with my first library book and simultaneously my love for the written word. You were my first home, my first safe place, and you continue to be to this day. Thank you for your ceaseless support and showing everyone who is lucky enough to be in your life what it truly is to be a friend.

Lisa Crosby, you have been a cheerleader through this whole thing. I honestly can't thank you enough. People underestimate the need for enthusiasm and curiosity, which you've given unreservedly. You were always ready to listen to my mounting uncertainty over burned coffee and custard pastries. Thank you for your insight and reminding me of the bigger picture.

To my brothers, Brian, Martin, and Paddy. Finally, something to rest your tea on and level out the dodgy table. Thank you for all the laughs, the care, the memes, the gusto, and the big-brother pride for your "baby sister."

To my parents. Mum, I don't think there's a cashier in Louth that's unaware I've written a book—and the shelves' worth of pre-orders have gone down really well with the publishers. Dad, I attribute so much of what I've been able to accomplish to your endless generosity and consistently prioritizing the happiness of your children over all else. I don't take it for granted. Thank you both for absolutely everything.

Adam and Ben, there's no Pokémon in here but in ten years' time it may have something that piques your interest. If not, see above for some examples on how your uncles may be using the book. I plan on gifting this regardless for a few decades to come.

Ger Minogue, I wouldn't be the me I am without you. You changed my life as I'm sure you have and will countless others. You are the spine of this book. From the bottom of my heart, thank you.

Áine Moriarty, you were the first person I told that someday I wanted to be an author. You believed seven-year-old me and continued to ask about the pending novel ever since. Thank you for your friendship—without you, things would have been very different. We're oceans away from each other, but I carry you in my heart every day.

Ann Gleeson, I can't imagine getting through training and beyond without having you there. You are the cure to all research malaise! Thank you for the guidance, the bellyaches, and the whiskey nights. I wouldn't be in this position without you. Becky Kehoe, I'd need a book in itself to detail everything I want to thank you for, but I'll keep it short and sweet: Thank you, gumdrop, I love you so much! Aisling Hoey, this isn't exactly *Jurassic Mart* but I hope you think it's *carbáge* all the same (I promise when that beauty takes off, the dedication will be entirely yours). Wil Wright, thank you for your dependability, your steadiness, your wit, and most of all, for moving back to Dublin. That was a bleak year. Never do that again.

Marie and Eliza Kennelly, two of the greatest tonics. Your support means the world. I'm forever grateful to have you both in my life and to now be able to call you family.

Sarah Williams, my book agent. Where do I start with this one?! Without you, this wouldn't have transpired anywhere *near* as well as it has (understatement of the century)! You are pure magic, and I'm so happy you took a risk on me.

Zennor Compton, thank you for the pools of patience, your keen eye, your wisdom, your reassurance—and for not running a mile upon receiving the first draft. To the entire team at Cornerstone, you handled every snippet written with the utmost care and attention. Thank you for taking my words and giving them a home.

To every single mind following @TheMindGeek on Instagram who made the account what it is. Every like, share, comment, follow…It hasn't gone unnoticed or unappreciated. You are as much a part of this book as I am. And yes, I still can't believe this has happened.

And last but by no means least, to Missy. I know everyone believes their dog is the greatest, but you really were. You showed me what it is to be loved boundlessly. May we all know what it is to feel such love. I count myself lucky to have been at the front row of your life. You were there for all the milestones and it's tricky not having you here for this one. Thank you for your eighteen years. I miss you girl, every day.

INDEX

Page references in *italics* indicate images.

ABOUT THE AUTHOR

SARAH CROSBY is a psychotherapist based in Dublin, Ireland. During her training, Sarah began creating and posting mental health content to Instagram as @TheMindGeek. The aim of her content is to make mental health information accessible and interesting, while occasionally delivering hard truths in soft colors. *Pocket Therapy* is her first book.